René Descartes

Meditations on First Philosophy

*In which the Existence of God
and the Distinction of the Human
Soul from the Body are Demonstrated*

A MONOLINGUAL EDITION

Edited, Translated and
Introduced by
George Heffernan

UNIVERSITY OF WOLVERHAMPTON
LIBRARY

Acc No.	CLASS
821028	194
CONTROL	DES
DATE 17. MAR. 1993	SITE D-/

UNIVERSITY OF NOTRE DAME PRESS
NOTRE DAME   LONDON

UNIVERSITY OF
WOLVERHAMPTON
DUDLEY CAMPUS LIBRARY

© 1992
University of Notre Dame Press
Notre Dame, Indiana 46556
All Rights Reserved
Manufactured in the United States of America

Library of Congress Cataloging-in-Publication Data

Descartes, René, 1596–1650
    [Meditationes de prima philosophia. English]
    Meditations on first philosophy : in which the ex-
istence of God and the distinction of the human soul
from the body are demonstrated / René Descartes :
edited, translated, and introduced by George Heffernan. — A monolingual ed.
        p.   cm.
    Translation of: Meditationes de prima philosophia.
    Includes bibliographical references.
    ISBN 0-268-01397-7 (pbk.)
    1. First philosophy—Early works to 1800. 2. God
—Proof, Ontological—Early works to 1800. 3. Meth-
odology—Early works to 1800. 4. Knowledge, Theory of—Early works to 1800. I. Heffernan, George.
II. Title.
B1853.E5H44   1992
194—dc20   91-50569
                                              CIP

CONTENTS

PREFACE TO THE MONOLINGUAL EDITION

This edition of Descartes' *Meditations on First Philosophy* is the monolingual edition of: René Descartes, *Meditationes de prima philosophia/Meditations on First Philosophy, A Bilingual Edition*, Introduced, Edited, Translated and Indexed by George Heffernan (Notre Dame/London: University of Notre Dame Press, 1990).

The bilingual edition has a much longer and more technical introduction, the original Latin text of the *Meditationes*, an index to the Latin text and a more extensive bibliography.

Since in the monolingual edition it is impossible to give the Adam and Tannery pagination exactly, it has not been given at all. Instead, the paragraphs of the Adam and Tannery edition have been numbered in square brackets for easy reference. As a rule, the text is cited and quoted much more precisely by paragraph than by page anyway.

In addition, the translation of the monolingual edition contains a few more commas and a small number of changes of word order vis-à-vis the bilingual one. Otherwise, the translations are essentially the same.

Finally, the introduction to the monolingual edition has been written keeping in mind that the edition will be used primarily to introduce undergraduate students to philosophy, theory of knowledge and Descartes. On the other hand, this introduction is also intended to be philosophically interesting to colleagues, showing, as I think it does, that Gettier was not at all "the first philosopher to see that the traditional definition of knowledge [as 'justified true belief'] is thus inadequate".

Here I would like to thank — besides those who have already been mentioned in the introduction to the bilingual edition — my colleagues at Merrimack College for the Faculty Development Grant awarded to me for the summer of 1991.

As was the bilingual edition, the present edition of the *Meditations* is dedicated to my former colleagues, the members of the Department of Philosophy of the University of Notre Dame: "...nam nihil accidere bono viro mali potest...".

And, last but not least, I thank Doris Hecker, Klaus Dieter Schönecker and Sylvia Ruschin for their *Gastfreundlichkeit*. Also, Herr Schönecker, a student of Gettier, challenged me to give a Gettier-like example from Descartes' *Meditations*. I refer to the description of "phantom pain" (VI, §§ 7 and 19–23). Suppose, like Chisholm, that

S *knows* that she is experiencing pain in her foot if and only if:
  (1) It is *true* that S is experiencing pain in her foot.
  (2) S *believes* that she is experiencing pain in her foot.
  (3) S is *justified* in believing that she is experiencing pain in her foot because she has ("adequate") evidence for it.
But further suppose, like Descartes, that:
  (4) It is true that S is experiencing pain in her foot, to be sure, *because* she is experiencing "*phantom* pain" "in" her foot.
  (5) S believes that it is true that she is experiencing pain in her foot, however, *because* she believes that she is experiencing pain *in* her foot.

So S *truly and justifiably believes* that she is experiencing pain "in" her foot, yet one cannot say — without further ado — that S "*knows*" that she is experiencing pain *in* her foot (which S *knows* has been *amputated*). Such cases motivated Descartes to write the *Meditations*, and they make one wonder about the definition of "knowledge" as "justified true belief".

Bonn, Summer Semester 1991   George Heffernan
Andover, Autumn Semester 1991

INTRODUCTION TO RENÉ DESCARTES'
MEDITATIONS ON FIRST PHILOSOPHY

In the *Meditations on First Philosophy, in which the Existence of God and the Distinction of the Human Soul from the Body are Demonstrated*, René Descartes seeks to ground knowledge in ("adequate") evidence by demonstrating the validity of "the general rule of truth",[1] that is, *that all the things that one clearly and distinctly perceives are true in that very manner in which one perceives them.*[2] Clarity and distinctness being modes of evidence, the main epistemic topic of the *Meditations* is a solution to the problem of the connection between ("adequate") evidence and truth or a solution to the problem of knowledge. In other words, Descartes' primary epistemic concern is with the proof of the *universality* and *necessity* of the connection between the clarity and distinctness of perceptions, on the one hand, and the truth of them, on the other hand, or with whether ("adequate") evidence *universally* and *necessarily* yields knowledge. Thus an answer must be found to the question as to whether Descartes really does prove *that everything that one clearly and distinctly perceives is true in that very manner in which one perceives it*, and any attempt to evaluate the epistemic foundationalism of the *Meditations* is inadequate if it does not recognize that the main claim thereof is that "the general rule of truth" is indeed "demonstrated".

But *why* try to establish an *absolutely* reliable connection between ("adequate") evidence and knowledge? *Why* attempt to argue that whatever one ("adequately") evidentially perceives

1

to be true must *necessarily* be true and cannot *possibly* be false? Well, *on the one hand*, there is the so-called "traditional definition of 'knowledge'" as "justified true belief", according to which one says — without further ado — that

S *knows* that P is true if and only if:
  (1)   P is *true*,
  (2)   S *believes* that P is true, and
  (3)   S is *justified* in believing that P is true because S has ("adequate") evidence for P.[3]

On the other hand, there is a recent critique of this definition, according to which one might propose, for example, cases of the following type:[4]

Jurors A-L *know* that it is true that M is a murderer if and only if:
  (1)   It is *true* that M is a murderer.
  (2)   Jurors A-L *believe* that it is true that M is a murderer.
  (3)   Jurors A-L are *justified* in believing that it is true that M is a murderer because they have ("adequate") evidence for it.
At which point would be added the further qualifications that:
  (4)   It is true that M is a murderer, to be sure, *because* M has murdered N.
  (5)   Jurors A-L believe that it is true that M is a murderer, however, *because* they believe that M has murdered O.[5]

Here, because someone "justifiably" — say the circumstantial and character evidence really and truly is convincing and persuasive ("adequate") — believes *the right thing*, but for *a wrong reason*, one would *not* want to speak of "knowledge".[6] Therefore "knowledge" does *not* appear to be "justified true belief" — at least not without further ado.

By the same token, Descartes is *not at all* convinced that "knowledge" can — again: *without further ado* — be defined in the "traditional" way as "true belief justified by ('adequate')

evidence". For in the *Meditations* he, too, mentions cases in which, *to be sure*, (1) P is *true*, (2) S *believes* that P is true, and (3) S is *justified* in believing that P is true because S has ("adequate") evidence for P, in which, *however*, one *cannot* say *without qualification* that "S *knows* that P is true".[7] Namely, under the topic of the epistemic *dualism* of the *distinction* between "the light of nature" and "the teaching of nature" — the radically *different* sources of natural "knowledge" — Descartes deals with the *discrepancy* between ("adequate") evidence and knowledge in some detail.[8] On the Cartesian description of the human being as a composite (*compositus*) of thinking thing (*res cogitans*) and extended thing (*res extensa*), there are many things (1) which are *true*, (2) which the human being *believes* are true, and (3) which the human being is *justified* in believing to be true because she has ("adequate") evidence for them, but which the human being may hardly be said *without qualification* "*to know*": for example, that the human being is healthy when she senses pleasure or ill when she senses pain, that she needs food or drink when she suffers hunger or thirst, that she is affected by some things accommodating or other things incommodious, that pleasant things are to be pursued and painful things are to be avoided, etc.[9] *According to the criteria of "the teaching of nature"*, the human being (*as a composite*) is so constituted as to *believe* both *truly* and *("adequately") evidentially* that such things are true, while, *according to the criteria of "the light of nature"*, she (*as a thinking thing*) cannot simply be said "*to know*" that they are true — *in particular*.

Thus it is *skepticism* with respect to the *reliability* of the relationship between ("adequate") evidence, on the one hand, and knowledge and truth, on the other hand, that *motivates* Descartes to seek to qualify ("adequate") "evidence" in such a way that it be *not seeming, but real, not deceptive, but genuine*, and *not insufficient, but fulfilling* — succeeding, he claims, with respect to "the light of nature", yet failing, he concedes, with respect to "the teaching of nature". So the main epistemic aim of the *Meditations* is to demonstrate that a *guarantee* can be given for the relationship between ("adequate") evidence, on the one hand, and knowledge and truth, on the other hand.

But order requires an overview of *the principal arguments* of the *Meditations*: Meditation I pretends to argue that, for valid and meditative reasons, essentially every belief (albeit not extensionally) is doubtful.[10] Meditation II argues, among other things, that "I think, therefore, I am" ("... cogito, ergo sum ..."), that is, that from thence that I think, it necessarily follows that I am:[11]

First Premiss:	If I (am) think(ing), then I am. — Doubt
Second Premiss:	But I (am) think(ing). factual
Conclusion:	Therefore I am.[12]

Among other things, Meditation III argues, first, that:

First Premiss:	I am.
Second Premiss:	And I have an idea of God.
Conclusion:	Therefore God exists.[13]

Then, that:

First Premiss:	All that which I very clearly and distinctly perceive is true.
Second Premiss:	But the idea of God that I have is that idea which is perceived maximally clearly and distinctly of all the ideas that I have.
Conclusion:	Therefore the idea of God that I have is that idea which is the maximally true idea of all the ideas that I have.[14]

And, finally, that:

First Premiss:	God is a perfect being.
Second Premiss:	But deception implies imperfection.
Conclusion:	Therefore God has nothing to do with deception.[15]

Meditation IV argues, among other things, that:

First Premiss:	God is the author of all clear and distinct perceptions.

Second Premiss:	But God is not a deceiver.
Conclusion:	Therefore every clear and distinct perception is true.[16]

Meditation V argues, among other things, that:

First Premiss:	God is a perfect being, whose essence is to possess all perfections.
Second Premiss:	But existence is a perfection.
Conclusion:	Therefore God exists.[17]

Meditation VI argues, among other things, that:

First Premiss:	"The light of nature" shows me that "the teaching of nature" informs me that the ideas of sensible things in me come from sensible things themselves outside me.
Second Premiss:	But God, the giver of "the light of nature" and "the teaching of nature", is not a deceiver.
Conclusion:	Therefore corporeal things exist.[18]

For obvious reasons, each argument is given in the respective short form.

In addition to the arguments of the individual meditations, there is also *the architectonic argument* concerning "the general rule of truth". For Descartes announces from the start of the *Meditations* that he intends "to prove"[19] or "to demonstrate"[20] the validity of "the general rule of truth"[21] *that whatever one (very) clearly and (very) distinctly perceives must necessarily be true and cannot possibly be false.* Caution is exercised in this matter, to be sure, at the beginning of Meditation III, since, *not yet* having "proved" it at this point, he is *not yet* justified in saying anything more than that "and *so I now seem to be able to establish* as a general rule that all that which I very clearly and distinctly perceive is true".[22] This does *not* prevent Descartes, however, from *presupposing* the validity of "the general rule of truth" in the proof for the existence of

God in that same meditation, for there, anticipating the objection that the idea of God upon which the argument depends, although it might be clear and distinct, could be false, he counters that this is impossible *because* this idea is the maximally clear and distinct idea, and, *therefore*, the maximally true idea, of all ideas.[23] The "demonstration" of the validity of "the general rule of truth" is in Meditation IV,[24] for *at the end of that meditation* Descartes states the "proof" for "the general rule of truth".[25] So the "demonstration" of the validity of "the general rule of truth" occurs *between the first proof for the existence of God* in Meditation III *and the second proof for the existence of God* in Meditation V. Throughout, the foundations of Cartesian foundationalism are — *directly, immediately and primarily* — "the natural light (of reason)" and — *indirectly, mediately and ultimately* — God as the giver of that light.[26] Here *light* is a *metaphor* for *evidence*, for which Descartes has no *concept* in the *Meditations*.

Naturally readers of the *Meditations* would object that here Descartes is arguing in a "circle", namely, by *first* using certain clear and distinct ideas or perceptions *in particular* to attempt to establish the truth of the claim that God exists, and by *then* turning around and appealing to God to try to substantiate the claim that all clear and distinct ideas or perceptions *in general* are true. This is one way of formulating the problem of "the Cartesian circle", that is, *that one can know that whatever one clearly and distinctly perceives is true if and only if one is certain that God exists and that he is not a deceiver, on the one hand, and that one can know that God exists and that he is not a deceiver if and only if one is certain that whatever one clearly and distinctly perceives is true, on the other hand.*

Is there a "(*vicious*) circle" here? Well, there is *only one* place in the *Meditations* where the word "circle" is used in the logical sense, namely, in the context of the question of how best to demonstrate to atheists that God exists.[27] There Descartes points out that one *cannot* rationally argue to atheists *both* that the existence of God is to be believed in *because* it is taught in Sacred Scripture *and* — vice versa — that Sacred Scripture is to be believed in *because* it is taught by God, since they would judge this to be a "circle". Obviously, they would not be the only ones, for this is a "circle" for anyone, believer as well as unbeliever, who makes use of the natural light of reason. This is a point which Descartes, who is here trying to present the *Meditations* as a piece of Christian apologetics, does not mention explicitly, let alone emphasize.[28]

But is it not also a "circle" to believe that God is reliable *because* the *Bible* says so, and — vice versa — that the *Bible* is reliable *because* God says so? "*If* the *Bible* is true, *then* God is good; and, *if* God is good, *then* the *Bible* is true." But *is* the *Bible true*? And *is* God *good*? Much is claimed, but little is argued. In the *Meditations* Descartes provides "a theological theory of evidence": "God" is mentioned 170 times,[29] but "evidence" *not once*.[30] So God is supposed to be even *more epistemically foundational* than ("adequate") evidence itself. But does this make (any) sense? For can evidence be validated by *anything but other, more and better evidence*?

The point is that the *Schlaraffenland* of a philosophy of knowledge without a philosophy of evidence exists only in the fairy-tale. For, if there can be *no knowledge without ("adequate") evidence*, then there can also be *no definition of "knowledge" without a definition of ("adequate") "evidence"*. In other words, if one *were* as serious about defining ("adequate") "evidence" as one *is* about defining "knowledge", then essays on the following model *would be* appropriate:

S has *("adequate") evidence* that P is true if and only if:
- (1)   ...?
- (2)   ...?
- (3)   ...?
- ...   ...?

For, *if* it is true that "nothing is older than the truth",[31] but that without ("adequate") evidence there is no knowledge of the truth, *then* it is also true that, with respect to knowledge of the truth, nothing is older than ("adequate") evidence.[32] And the assertion that there can be no definition or definite description of "knowledge" without a corresponding definition or definite description of ("adequate") "evidence" surely does *not* hold *only* for Descartes' *Meditations on First Philosophy*. ... [33]

NOTES

1 Cf. René Descartes (1596–1650), *Meditationes de prima philosophia*
. . . (1641/42), *Oeuvres de Descartes*, ed. Charles Adam and Paul Tannery,
Vol. VII (Paris 1904), Meditation III, § 2 ("a general rule"), and V, § 15
("this rule of truth").

2 Cf., e.g., "Synopsis", §§ 2 and 4, I, §§ 9–12, II, §§ 3 and 6, III,
§§ 2, 4, 9, 16, 25 and 38, IV, §§ 1–2, 10, 12 and 15–17, V, §§ 6–7
and 11–15, VI, §§ 6–7, 9–10, 11–16 and 23–24, etc.

3 Cf., e.g., Roderick Chisholm, *Theory of Knowledge* (Englewood
Cliffs, N.J., 1966, 1977, 1989), pp. 90–100 (of the Third Edition). With
each new edition of *Theory of Knowledge* there was more and more "ado"
about the definition of "knowledge" as "justified true belief".

4 This example from "true crime" is inspired by the *legal* distinction
between *direct* and *indirect* evidence.

5 Cf. Edmund Gettier, "Is Justified True Belief Knowledge?", *Analysis*, Vol. 23 (1963), pp. 121–123. For some rather odd reason, Gettier is
generally regarded — at least in certain ahistorical, analytic circles — as
"the first philosopher to see that the traditional definition of knowledge
is thus inadequate" (Chisholm, *op. cit.*, p. 92).

6 Not all Gettier-type examples require this kind of belief based on a
false assumption: cf., e.g., Richard Feldman, "An Alleged Defect in Gettier
Counter-Examples", *Australasian Journal of Philosophy*, Vol. 52 (1974),
pp. 68–69. But efforts are underway, or so one is assured, to take care of
those that do not, too: cf., e.g., Chisholm, *op. cit.*, pp. 91–99.

7 A *careful* reading of the *Theaetetus* — from which "the traditional
definition of 'knowledge' " as "justified true belief" is, by the way, supposed to derive — shows that *already* Plato and Socrates do *not* think that
the conditions given are *sufficient* for knowledge (cf., e.g., 200 d-201 c
and 201 c-210 b). This interpretation is compossible with: Myles Burnyeat,
The "Theaetetus" of Plato (Indianapolis/Cambridge 1990), pp. 128–241.

8 Cf. the references to "the light of nature" and "the teaching of nature" in the Index of: René Descartes, *Meditationes de prima philosophia/
Meditations on First Philosophy, A Bilingual Edition*, Introduced, Edited,
Translated and Indexed by George Heffernan (Notre Dame/London 1990),
pp. 219–246.

9 Cf., e.g., VI, §§ 6–23, on *deception* by *particulars*.

10 Cf. esp. "Synopsis", § 1, I, §§ 9–12, III, § 4, VI, § 24, etc.

11 Cf. §§ 3 and 6 (cf. III, § 9, IV, § 10, etc.). The classic formulation
itself does *not* occur in the *Meditations*.

12 There are many different ways to state this argument, and there are
difficulties with all of them.

13 Deliberately brief and bold: cf. the summary of the argument for
the existence of God in § 36 (and III, § 38, IV, § 1, etc.).

14 Cf. III, §§ 2 and 25. The claim of the second premiss is perhaps even more provocative than that of the first.

15 Cf. the argument formulated in § 38 (cf. IV, § 2). But what *argument* is given that God is good or perfect?

16 Cf. the argument of § 17. The claim of the first premiss is not as hard *to understand* as it seems to be.

17 Cf. the argument of §§ 7–12. The issue is, of course, whether "existence" is a "perfection" and-or a "predicate".

18 Cf. the argument of § 10, i.e., the argument for the existence of the external world.

19 Cf. "Synopsis", §§ 2 and 4.

20 Cf. V, § 6.

21 Cf. again III, § 2, and V, § 15.

22 Cf. III, § 2 (italics added).

23 Cf. III, § 25 — one of the most important paragraphs of the *Meditations*, especially for the "circle".

24 Cf. "Synopsis", § 4.

25 Cf. again IV, § 17.

26 Cf. "Synopsis", § 4, III, §§ 9, 14–15, 20, 28, 31, 38–39, IV, §§ 12–13, VI, § 15, etc.

27 Cf. "Dedicatory Epistle", § 1.

28 Cf. ibid., § 3.

29 Cf. the Index to the bilingual edition, p. 226.

30 The word "evidentia" does *not* occur *once* in the *Meditations* *proper* (but cf. "Dedicatory Epistle", § 5).

31 Cf. *Meditations*, "Dedicatory Epistle", § 4: ". . . nihil est veritate antiquius . . . ".

32 Leibniz' study *Meditationes de cognitione, veritate et ideis* (*Meditations on Knowledge, Truth and Ideas*) (1684) is and remains *the* classic analysis of the vulnerability gap between ("adequate") evidence, on the one hand, and knowledge and truth, on the other hand. The main thesis is that "perfect" knowledge is as rare as "adequate" evidence, i.e., *very* rare indeed.

33 Admittedly, because "adequate" can mean "satisfying" (weak sense) or "saturating" (strong sense), the expression "adequate evidence" is *equivocal*. Thus some proceed from one notion of adequacy and argue *that there can be adequate evidence without knowledge* (e.g., the Husserl of the *Logical Investigations* [1900–01/1913–21]), while others proceed from another notion of adequacy and argue *that there can be knowledge without adequate evidence* (e.g., the Husserl of the *Formal and Transcendental Logic* [1929]). Which ("adequate") evidence is (*really*) "adequate" for knowlege? Still, one cannot eat one's cake and have it, too, that is, it is wrong and unfair *both* to affirm that Plato, Descartes, *et al.* think that "knowledge" is "justified true belief" *and* to deny that they are aware of the difficulties with this so-called "traditional definition of 'knowledge' ".

RENÉ
DESCARTES,
MEDITATIONS
ON FIRST
PHILOSOPHY,
IN WHICH THE EXISTENCE OF GOD
AND THE IMMORTALITY OF THE SOUL
ARE DEMONSTRATED.
PARIS,

By MICHAEL SOLY, James Street, under

the sign of the Phoenix.

1641.

*With the Privilege, & the Approbation
of the Doctors.*

RENÉ
DESCARTES,
MEDITATIONS
On First
PHILOSOPHY,

In which the existence of God,
& the distinction of the human soul from the body,
are demonstrated.

To which have been added various objections of
learned men against these demonstrations
concerning God and the soul;

With the Responses of the Author.

Second edition, enlarged by the previously
unpublished seventh objections.

Amsterdam,
By Ludwig Elzevir. 1642.

[DEDICATORY EPISTLE]

TO THOSE MOST WISE AND DISTINGUISHED MEN,

THE DEAN AND THE DOCTORS

OF THE SACRED FACULTY OF THEOLOGY AT PARIS,

RENÉ DESCARTES SAYS "GREETINGS".

[1.] So just a cause impels me to offer this writing to you, and I trust that you, too, are going to have such a just one for taking up its defence — after you will have understood the reason for my undertaking —, that I could here commend it by no better means than if I were to say with a few words what I have pursued in it.

[2.] Of the questions that need to be demonstrated by philosophy rather than theology I have always thought that two, about God and about the soul, are foremost. For, although it might suffice for us faithful to believe by faith that the human soul does not perish with the body and that God exists, it certainly seems that no religion — nor almost even any moral virtue — can persuade unbelievers unless these two things were first proved to them by natural reason. And, since in this life greater rewards often be offered to vices than to virtues, few people would prefer what is right to what is useful if they did not fear God or expect another life. And, although it might be quite true that the existence of God is to be believed in because it is taught in the Holy Scriptures and — vice versa — that the Holy Scriptures are to be believed in because they are had from God — because, since faith be a gift of God, he, the same one who gives the grace to believe the other things, can, of course, also give it to us in order that we might believe that he exists —, this still cannot be proposed to unbelievers, because they would judge that it is a circle. And I have surely noticed

13

not only that you and all the other theologians affirm that the existence of God can be proved by natural reason, but also that it is inferred from the Holy Scriptures that the cognition of him is easier than many cognitions which are had of created things, and indeed that it is so easy that those people who do not have it be at fault. For this is obvious from these words in *Wisdom*, chapter 13: "Nor should it be forgiven them. For, if they have been able to know so much that they could value the world, why have they not more easily found its Lord?" And in *To the Romans*, chapter 1, it is said that these people are "inexcusable". And in the same place, by these words, " . . . what is known of God is manifest in them . . . ", we also seem to be warned that all the things that can be known about God can be shown by reasoning drawn from nowhere else than from our mind itself. Therefore, I have not thought it to be alien to me to inquire into how this might be done, and by which way God might be cognized more easily and more certainly than the things of the world.

[3.] And, as for the soul, even if many people may have judged that its nature cannot easily be investigated, and even if some people may have even dared to say that human reasoning persuades us that it perishes together with the body and that the contrary is held by faith alone, because the Lateran Council held under Leo X in Session 8 condemns these people and expressly mandates to Christian philosophers that they should dissolve the arguments of them and prove the truth according to their abilities, I have still not hesitated to attempt this, too.

[4.] Moreover, because I know that most impious people do not want to believe that there is a God and that the human mind is distinguished from the body for any other reason than because, they say, these two things have hitherto been able to be demonstrated by no one — even if I would in no way agree with them, but rather would I — on the contrary — think that almost all the arguments that have been brought forward for these questions by great men then have the force of demonstration when they are satisfactorily understood, and I might hardly persuade myself that any arguments can be given which had not been found earlier by some others —, I still think that nothing more useful can have priority in philosophy than if once and for all the best of all the arguments be inquired into studiously and be set out so accurately and perspicuously that in posterity it might be a constant for all people that they are demonstrations. And, finally, because some people to whom it is known that I have developed a certain method for resolving whatever difficulties there are in the sciences — surely not a new method, for nothing is older than the truth, but one which they have seen me often use not infelicitously in other things — strongly urged this of me, I have, therefore, thought it to be my duty to attempt to accomplish something in this matter.

[5.] Furthermore, whatever I have been able to achieve is all contained in this treatise. Not that I had attempted to collect in it all the different arguments which could be put forward to prove the same things, for, except where none is held to be certain enough, this does not seem to be worth the effort. Rather have I prosecuted only the first and foremost arguments, so that I would now dare to propose these as very certain and very evident demonstrations. And I would even add that these demonstrations are such that I would not think that there is any way open to the human mind by which better ones could ever be found. For the necessity of the cause and the glory of God — to which this whole thing is referred — here force me to speak about the things that pertain to me somewhat more freely than my custom brings me to do. Yet, however much certain and evident that you will I might think these demonstrations to be, I still cannot therefore persuade myself that they have been accommodated to the capacity of all people. Rather, just as in geometry many demonstrations have been written by Archimedes, Apollonius, Pappus and others which, even if they be held by all people to be evident and also certain because they indeed contain nothing at all which — regarded with respect to itself — would not be very easy to cognize and nothing in which consequent things would not accurately cohere with antecedent ones, because they are somewhat long and require a very attentive reader, are still understood by only very few people: so also, even if I would consider the demonstrations that I use here to equal or even to surpass geometrical ones with respect to certitude and evidence, I still fear that they could not satisfactorily be perceived by many people, both because they, too, are somewhat long and some depend on others and, above all, because they require a mind fully free from prejudices and one that might easily withdraw itself from the company of the senses. Certainly not more people are found in the world fit for metaphysical studies than for geometrical ones. And, moreover, there is a difference in that in geometry, since all people have been persuaded that usually nothing is written of which a certain demonstration not be had, the inexperienced people err more often in that they would accept false things while they want to seem to understand them than in that they would reject true things: but in philosophy, on the contrary, since it is believed that there is nothing that could not be disputed on either side, few people investigate the truth and many more pursue fame of mind from thence that they would dare to attack whatever optimal things there are.

[6.] And, therefore, whatever the quality of my arguments might be, because they have to do with philosophy, I still do not expect that I am going to accomplish very valuable work by means of them unless you would support me by your patronage. But, since there is so great an opinion of your Faculty in the minds of all people and the name of the "Sorbonne" is of so great authority that not only in matters of faith no society after the Sacred Councils has ever been believed so much as yours, but also in human philosophy there is nowhere else thought to be more perspicacity and solidity nor more integrity and wisdom in rendering judgment, I do not doubt that, if you would deign to give so much care to this writing — namely, *first*, in order that it might be corrected by you, for, remembering not only my humanity, but also, maximally, my ignorance, I do not affirm that there are no errors in it, *then*, in order that the things that are lacking or are not satisfactorily absolute or require more explication might be added, perfected or illustrated either by you yourselves or at least by me, after I will have been warned by you, and, *finally*, in order that, after the arguments contained in it, by means of which it is proved that there is a God and that the mind is other than the body, will have been led through to that perspicuity through to which, I am confident, they can be led, so that thus they might, of course, be held to be very accurate demonstrations, you might want to declare and to attest publicly to this very thing —, I do not doubt, I say, that, if this were to happen, then all the errors which there have ever been on these questions would soon be deleted from the minds of human beings. For the truth itself will easily effect that the other ingenious and learned people would subscribe to your judgment, and authority will easily effect that the atheists, who are usually more pretenders than ingenious or learned, would lay down the spirit of contradiction and also that they themselves would perhaps fight for these arguments, which they will know to be held to be demonstrations by all people gifted of mind, so that they might not seem not to understand the arguments. And, finally, all the other people will easily believe so many testimonies and there will be no one in the world any longer who would dare to call into doubt the existence of God or the real distinction of the human soul from the body. By virtue of your singular wisdom you can estimate best of all yourselves how great be the utility of this matter. Nor would it become me to commend to you, who have always been the greatest pillar of the Catholic Church, the cause of God and religion with any more words here.

PREFACE TO THE READER

[1.] I have already a few years ago touched on the questions of God and the human mind in the *Discourse on the Method of correctly Conducting the Reason and of Investigating the Truth in the Sciences*, published in French in the year 1637, surely not in order that I might there treat of them accurately, but only in order that I might offer a sampling of my views and discern from the judgments of the readers how they were to be treated of later on. For these questions have seemed to me to be of such importance that I would judge that with them is to be dealt more than one time, and I follow a way of explicating them so little trodden and so remote from the common usage that I had thought it to be not useful to teach it in more detail in a writing in French and in one to be read by all people without distinction, so that the weaker minds could not believe that it is to be taken by them, too.

[2.] But, although I have there requested of all those people to whom there would occur something in my writings worthy of reprehension that they might deign to warn me of it, nothing worthy of notice has been objected to the things on which I had touched of these questions except for two matters, to which I shall here respond with a few words before I go on to a more accurate explication of the same things.

[3.] The first thing is that from thence that the human mind — turned towards itself — were not to perceive itself to be anything other than a cogitating thing, it does not follow that its nature or *essence* consists only therein that it be a cogitating thing, so that the word "only" would exclude all the other things which could perhaps also be said to pertain to the nature of the soul. To which objection I respond that there I, too, have not wanted to exclude these things in the order of the truth itself of the matter (with which, scil., I was not then dealing), but rather only in the order of my perception, so that the sense were that I cognized nothing at all that I were to know to pertain to my essence except that I were a cogitating thing, or a thing having in itself the faculty of cogitating. In the following meditations, however, I shall show how from thence that I were to cognize that nothing else pertains to my essence, it would also follow that nothing else really and truly pertains to it.

[4.] The other thing is that from thence that I were to have in me an idea of a thing more perfect than me, it does not follow that this idea itself is more perfect than me, and much less that that which is represented by this idea exists. But I respond that here there is an equivocation hidden in the word "idea": for it can be taken materially, as an operation of the intellect, in which sense it cannot be called "more perfect than me"; or it can be taken objectively, as the thing represented by this operation, which thing — even if it were not to be supposed to exist outside the intellect — can still be more perfect than me by reason of its essence. Yet in the following meditations it will be set forth in detail how from thence alone that the idea of a thing more perfect than me be in me, it would follow that this thing really and truly exists.

[5.] Moreover, I have indeed seen two rather long writings, by which, however, not so much my reasoning concerning these matters, as rather my conclusions were attacked with arguments borrowed from the common places in the texts of the atheists. And, because arguments of this kind can have no force for those people who will understand my reasoning, and because the judgments of many people are so preposterous and weak that they be persuaded more by opinions at first accepted — however much that you will false and alien to reason — than by a refutation of them true and firm — but heard later on —, I do not want to respond to these arguments here, so that they not first be referred to by me. And I would only generally say that all the things that are commonly thrown about by the atheists to attack the existence of God always depend thereupon that human emotions be feigned of God or thereupon that so much power and wisdom be arrogated to our minds that we would try to determine and to comprehend what God could and should do. So long as we would only just remember that our minds are to be considered as finite, but that God is to be considered as incomprehensible and infinite, these things are going to cause us no difficulty.

[6.] But, after I have now gotten to know by experience, to a certain extent, the judgments of human beings, I here go on once again to the same questions about God and the human mind and simultaneously to treat of the initial things of the whole of First Philosophy. Yet I do so in such a way that I would expect no applause of the common people and no frequency of readers. Rather am I an author to none who might read these things except only to those people who will be able and willing to meditate seriously with me and to lead the mind simultaneously away from the senses and away from all prejudices: whom I know well enough to be very few. But, as for those people who — not caring to comprehend the order and the connection of my arguments — will attempt to argue only against individual formulations — as it is the custom for many —, they are not going to find the reading of this writing very fruitful. And, although these people might perhaps find occasion to cavil against many things, they will still not easily object something that would be urgent or worthy of a response.

[7.] But, because I also do not even promise that I am going to satisfy the other readers in all matters from the very first page, nor do I arrogate so much wisdom to myself that I would be confident that I can foresee all the things that will seem difficult to anyone, first I shall at least set out in the *Meditations* those cogitations themselves with the help of which I seem to me to have arrived at a certain and evident cognition of the truth, so that I might know by experience whether I could perhaps persuade other people, too, by the same arguments by which *I* have been persuaded. But I shall afterwards respond to the objections of some men, excellent with respect to mind and learning, to whom these *Meditations* have been sent to be examined before they were submitted to print. For the things objected to by these men have been many and varied enough that I would dare to hope it not to be easy that anything — at least anything of any importance — on which they had not already touched is going to come to mind for others. And, therefore, I also request of even the readers, too, that they would not render judgment on the *Meditations* before they had been kind enough to read through all these objections and their solutions.

SYNOPSIS
OF THE FOLLOWING SIX MEDITATIONS

[1.] *In the first Meditation, the reasons are set out due to which we can doubt all things, especially material ones — so long as, scil., we do not have foundations of the sciences other than the ones that we have had up until now. But, even if the utility of such great doubt would not be apparent at first sight, it is still maximal, in that it might free us from all prejudices and prepare a very easy way for leading the mind away from the senses; and, finally, it might effect that we could no longer doubt the things that we will afterwards find out to be true.*

[2.] *In the second Meditation, the mind, which — using its own freedom — supposes that all those things whose existence it can even at a minimum doubt do not exist, notices that it cannot happen that it itself would not exist during this time. Which is also of the greatest utility, because by this means the mind easily distinguishes between which things would pertain to it, that is, to an intellectual nature, and which things would pertain to the body.* But, because some people will perhaps expect arguments for the immortality of the soul in this place, I think that they are to be warned here that I have tried to write nothing that I would not accurately demonstrate, and, therefore, that I could have followed no other order than that which is usual with the geometers, so that I would, of course, set forth all the things on which the questioned proposition depends before I would conclude anything about it. Moreover, I think that they are to be warned here that the first and foremost thing which is prerequisite for cognizing the immortality of the soul is that we were to form a concept of it maximally perspicuous and plainly distinct from every concept of body, which has been done here. But, in addition, I think that they are to be warned here that it is also required that we were to know that all the things that we clearly and distinctly understand are true in that mode itself in which we understand them, which has not been able to be proved before the fourth Meditation; and that a distinct concept of corporeal nature is to be had, which is formed partly in the second Meditation itself and partly in the fifth and sixth Meditation; and that from these things it should be concluded that all the things that are clearly and distinctly conceived as different substances, as mind and body are conceived, really and truly are substances really mutually distinct from each other; and that this is concluded in the sixth Meditation. And I think that they are to be warned here that in the sixth Meditation the same thing is also confirmed from thence that we might understand no body except as being divisible, but — on the contrary — no mind except as being indivisible, for we cannot conceive of a half-part of any mind as we can conceive of a half-part of any body, however small that you will — so much so that the natures of mind and body be recognized not only as being different, but also as being in a certain manner contrary. But I think that they are to be warned here that I have not further dealt with this matter in this writing, *first, because these things suffice to show that from the corruption of the body the perishing of the mind does not follow — and thus to make hope to mortals of another life —, then, too, because the premises from which the immortality itself of the mind can be concluded depend on the explication of the whole of physics: first, that it be known that absolutely all substances — or things which must be created by God in order that they may exist — are by their nature incorruptible, nor can they ever cease to be unless they be reduced to nothing by the same God's denying his concurrence to them, and, then, that it be noticed that body — at least taken in general — is a substance and, therefore, that it, too, never perishes. But I think that they are to be warned here that the human body, in so far as it differs from other bodies, is not made up of anything except of a certain configuration of members and other accidents of this kind, yet that the human mind does not thus consist of any accidents, but rather is it a pure substance. For, even if all its accidents would change, so that it would understand other things, want other things, sense other things, etc., the mind itself does not therefore become another mind. But the human body becomes another body from thence alone that the figure of some of its parts were to change. From which things it follows that the body very easily indeed perishes, but that the mind is by its nature immortal.*

[3.] In the third Meditation, I have explicated in satisfactory detail — as it seems to me — my foremost argument for proving the existence of God. But, because there I have wanted to use no comparisons taken from corporeal things in order that I might maximally lead the minds of the readers away from the senses, many obscurities have perhaps still remained, which will, however, as I hope, fully be eliminated afterwards in the responses to the objections, obscurities such as, among others, how the idea of a most highly perfect being, which is in us, may have so much objective reality that it could not not be from a most highly perfect cause — which is there illustrated by the comparison with a very perfect machine of which the idea is in the mind of some artificer. For, just as the objective artifice must have some cause of the idea of it, namely, the scientific

knowledge of its artificer — or of someone else from whom he has received it —, so the idea of God which is in us cannot not have God himself as its cause.

[4.] *In the fourth Meditation, it is proved that all the things that we clearly and distinctly perceive are true and it is simultaneously explicated wherein the nature of falsity were to consist: which things should necessarily be known, as much to render firm the preceding things as to understand the remaining ones. (But it is to be noticed, however, that sin — or error that is committed in the pursuit of good and evil — is in no way dealt with there; rather is that error only which occurs in the judging of the true and the false dealt with there. Nor are the things regarded that pertain to faith or to the conduct of life, but rather are regarded only the truths that are speculative and cognized with the help of the natural light alone.)*

[5.] *In the fifth Meditation, in addition thereto that corporeal nature — taken in general — is explicated, the existence of God is also demonstrated by a new argument. But, again, perhaps there occur in it some difficulties, which will later be resolved in the response to the objections. And, finally, it is shown how it be true that the certitude of geometrical demonstrations themselves depends on the cognition of God.*

[6.] *In the sixth Meditation, finally, intellection is distinguished from imagination; the criteria of the distinctions are described; it is proved that the mind is really to be distinguished from the body; the mind is shown to be, nonetheless, so closely joined to the body that it might compose one thing with it; all the errors that usually arise from the senses are reviewed; the means by which these errors could be avoided are set out; and, finally, all the arguments from which the existence of material things could be concluded are brought forward: not that I would think these arguments to be very useful for proving that itself which they do prove, namely, that there really and truly is a world and that human beings have bodies and similar things — which no one of sane mind has ever seriously doubted —, but rather because by considering these arguments it is recognized that they are not as firm nor as perspicuous as are those arguments by which we arrive at the cognition of our own mind and*

of God — *so much so that these latter arguments be the most
certain and the most evident of all the arguments that could
be known by the human mind. Of which one thing I have proposed the proof as my goal in these Meditations. Nor, therefore,
do I here review those various other questions of which are also
occasionally treated in these Meditations.*

OF THE MEDITATIONS

ON FIRST

PHILOSOPHY

IN WHICH THE EXISTENCE OF GOD &
THE DISTINCTION OF THE SOUL FROM THE BODY
ARE DEMONSTRATED

THE FIRST

Concerning the things that can be called into doubt.

[1.] Already some years ago, I have noticed how many false things I, going into my youth, had admitted as true and how dubious were whatever things I have afterwards built upon them, and, therefore, that once in my life all things are fundamentally to be demolished and that I have to begin again from the first foundations, if I were to desire ever to stabilize something firm and lasting in the sciences. But the task seemed to be a huge one, and I waited for that age which would be so mature that none more fit for the disciplines to be pursued would follow. Thus I have delayed so long that I would now be at fault if by deliberating I were to consume that time which remains for what is to be done. Today, then, I have opportunely rid the mind of all cares and I have procured for myself secure leisure, I am withdrawing alone and, at last, I shall devote myself seriously and freely to this general demolition of my opinions.

[2.] To do this, however, it will not be necessary that I would show that all my opinions are false, which I could perhaps never achieve anyway. Because reason already persuades me that assent is to be withheld no less accurately from the opinions that are not fully certain and indubitable than from the ones that are overtly false, rather will it suffice to reject all my opinions if I shall have found any reason for doubting in each one. And, therefore, nor will these opinions have to be gone through individually, which would be an infinite task. But, because — the foundations having been undermined — whatever has been built upon them will collapse spontaneously, I will go right for those principles upon which rested all that which I have once believed.

[3.] Namely, whatever I have admitted up until now as maximally true I have accepted from the senses or through the senses. Yet I have found that these senses sometimes deceive me, and it is a matter of prudence never to confide completely in those who have deceived us even once.

[4.] But, even if the senses would perhaps sometimes deceive us about certain minute and more remote things, there are still many other things that plainly cannot be doubted, although they be derived from the same senses: such as that I am now here, that I am sitting by the fire, that I am clothed in a winter robe, that I am holding this piece of paper with the hands, and similar things. Truly, by means of what reasoning could it be denied that these hands themselves and this whole body are mine? Unless I were perhaps to compare myself with — I know not which — insane people, whose brains the stubborn vapor of black bile so weakens that they might constantly assert that they are kings when they are very poor, or that they are clothed in purple when they are nude, or that they have an earthenware head, or that they are — as wholes — pumpkins or made of glass. But these people are without minds, nor would I myself seem less demented if I were to transfer something as an example from them to me.

[5.] Brilliantly soundly argued, as if I were not a human being who would be accustomed to sleep at night and to undergo passively in dreams all the same things as — or even sometimes things less verisimilar than — those which these insane people then do when they are awake. Truly, how frequently nocturnal rest persuades me of such usual things — that I am here, that I am dressed in a robe, that I am sitting by the fire —, when, however, the clothes having been taken off, I am lying between the sheets! And yet now I certainly intuit this piece of paper with waking eyes. This head which I move is not asleep. As one who is prudent and knowing I extend this hand and I sense. Things so distinct would not happen to someone sleeping. As if, scil., I did not remember that on other occasions I have also been deluded in dreams by similar cogitations. While I cogitate these things more attentively, I see so plainly that being awake can never be distinguished from sleep by certain criteria that I be stupefied, and this stupor itself would almost confirm for me the opinion of being asleep.

[6.] So, therefore, we be dreaming. Neither would these particular things be true — that we open the eyes, move the head, extend the hands —, nor perhaps would it even be true that we have such hands or such a whole body. It is, in fact, still to be conceded that the things that are seen during sleep are like a kind of pictured images which cannot have been feigned except according to the similitude of true things. And hence it is, in fact, to be conceded that at least these general things — eyes, head, hands and the whole body — exist as a kind of things that are not imaginary, but rather true. For indeed painters themselves, even when they try to feign sirens and satyrs with maximally unusual forms, cannot then assign to them natures new with respect to every part, but rather can they only mix together the members of different animals. Or, if these painters were perhaps to excogitate something so very new that nothing at all similar to it had ever been seen — and it would thus be completely fictitious and false —, at a minimum the colors out of which they would compose it must certainly still be true. By not dissimilar reasoning, although these general things, too — eyes, head, hands and similar things — could be imaginary, it is still necessarily to be conceded that at least certain other things even more simple and universal are true: things even more simple and universal out of which — as from true colors — are feigned all those images of things which, whether true or false, are in our cogitation.

[7.] Of which kind seem to be corporeal nature in general, and its extension; also, the figure of extended things; also, the quantity, or the magnitude and the number of the same things; also, the place in which they may exist, and the time through which they may endure, and similar things.

[8.] Therefore, we will perhaps well conclude from these things that physics, astronomy, medicine and all the other disciplines that depend on the consideration of composite things are indeed dubious, but that arithmetic, geometry and the other disciplines of this kind — which treat only of the simplest and maximally general things and which care little about whether these would be in the nature of things or not — contain something certain and indubitable. For, whether I would be awake or sleeping, two and three added together are five, and a square has no more than four sides. Nor does it seem that it can happen that truths so perspicuous would incur the suspicion of falsity.

[9.] And yet there is fixed in my mind a certain old opinion that there is a God who can do all things and by whom I, as such as I exist, have been created. But how do I know that he has not made it so that there would be no earth at all, no heavens, no extended thing, no figure, no magnitude, no place, and yet that all these things would seem to me to exist not otherwise than they seem to now? And how do I even know that he has not made it so that I — just as I sometimes judge that other people err about the things that they think that they know most perfectly, so, too, I — would be deceived whenever I add two and three together, or count the sides of a square, or something else easier, if it can be imagined? But perhaps God has not willed to deceive me thus, for he is called "the most highly good". Yet, if this — to have created me such that I were always to be deceived — would contradict his goodness, it would also seem to be alien to the same goodness to permit that I were sometimes to be deceived: which last thing, however, cannot be said.

[10.] But there might perhaps be some people who would prefer to deny the existence of a God so powerful than to believe that all other things are uncertain. Yet let us not contradict them, and let us grant that all this about God is fictitious. On the other hand, these people might suppose that I have come by fate, or by chance, or by a continuous series of things, or by whatever other means that you will, to be that which I am. Because to be deceived and to err seem to be certain imperfections, the less powerful an author of my origin these people will assign, the more probable will it be that I am so imperfect that I would always be deceived. To which arguments I do not have anything that I might soundly respond, but rather am I forced, finally, to concede that of the things which I once held to be true there is none that it would not be permitted to doubt — and this not through lack of consideration or levity, but because of valid and meditative reasons. And, therefore, I am forced to concede that from now on assent is accurately to be withheld from the same things, too, no less than from the overtly false ones, if I would want to find something certain.

[11.] But to have noticed these things does not yet suffice; care is to be taken that I might remember them. For accustomed opinions assiduously recur, and almost even involuntarily for me do they occupy my credulity, which is bound to them as though by long use and the right of familiarity. Nor shall I ever break the habit of assenting to and confiding in these opinions, so long as I were to suppose that they are such as they really and truly are, namely, at least in a certain mode dubious, as has just been shown, but nonetheless very probable, and opinions that it would be much more consentaneous to reason to believe than to deny. Therefore, I am of the opinion that I would not do badly if — the will having been turned completely to the contrary — I were to deceive myself, and if I were to feign for a time that these opinions are entirely false and imaginary, until, finally, the weights of prejudices having been — as it were — balanced on both sides, no depraved custom would any longer detour my judgment from the correct perception of things. For I know that in the meantime no danger or error is going to follow therefrom, and that I cannot indulge in too much diffidence, since I am now occupied not with things to be done, but rather only with things to be cognized.

[12.] I shall, then, suppose that not the optimal God — the font of truth —, but rather some malign genius — and the same one most highly powerful and most highly cunning —, has put all his industriousness therein that he might deceive me: I shall think that the heavens, the air, the earth, colors, figures, sounds and all external things are nothing other than the playful deceptions of dreams by means of which he has set traps for my credulity; I shall consider myself as not having hands, not eyes, not flesh, not blood, not any senses, but rather as falsely opining that I have all these things; I shall obstinately remain as one fixed in this meditation, and, even if it would thus not be in my power to cognize something true, yet that which is in me is certainly that I shall with a firm mind be cautious that I were not to assent to false things, and that the deceiver — however powerful that you will, however cunning that you will — could not impose anything on me. But this undertaking is laborious, and a certain slothfulness reduces me to the custom of life. Not otherwise than a prisoner who perhaps enjoyed an imaginary freedom in a dream, and who, when he begins after a while to suspect that he is sleeping, then is afraid to be awakened and languidly connives with the agreeable illusions: thus do I spontaneously fall back into old opinions and fear waking up, lest the laborious wakefulness following the placid rest would in the future have to be spent not in some light, but rather among the inextricable shadows of the difficulties already raised.

MEDITATION II.

Concerning the nature of the human mind:
that it be more known than [the] body.

[1.] I have been thrown into so great doubts by yesterday's meditation that I could no longer forget them, nor would I yet see by means of what reasoning they were to be resolved. Rather, like one who has improvidently fallen into a deep whirlpool, I am so perturbed that I could neither fix a foot on the bottom nor swim to the top. I shall make an effort, however, and I shall once again attempt to go the way that I have gone yesterday, scil., by removing all that which admits of doubt even at a minimum, no less than if I had found it to be completely false. And I shall proceed further in this direction until I might cognize something certain, or — if nothing else — at least this itself for certain: that there is nothing certain. Archimedes demanded nothing but a point that be firm and immovable in order that he might move the entire earth from its place: great things are also to be hoped for if I shall have found even something minimal that be certain and unshakeable.

[2.] I am supposing, then, that all the things that I see are false; I believe that none of the things that the mendacious memory represents has ever existed; I have no senses at all; body, figure, extension, movement and place are chimeras. What will, then, be true? Perhaps just this one thing: that there is nothing certain.

[3.] But from whence do I know that there is nothing which is different from all the things that I have already reviewed and concerning which there were not even a minimal occasion of doubting? Is there not a "God" — or by whatever other name I would call him — who immits these cogitations themselves into me? But why would I think this, since I myself could perhaps be the author of them? Am *I* not, therefore, at least something?

31

Yet I have already denied that I have any senses and any body.
I pause, however; for what follows from thence? Am I not so
bound to the body and to the senses that I could not be without
them? But I have persuaded myself that there is nothing at all in
the world, no heavens, no earth, no minds, no bodies: also, then,
that I am not? No, if I was persuading myself of something, then
certainly *I* was. Yet there is a deceiver — I know not who he is
—, most highly powerful and most highly cunning, who always
industriously deceives me. If he is deceiving me, then without
doubt *I* also am; and he might deceive me as much as he can,
he will still never effect that I would be nothing, so long as I
shall be cogitating that I am something. So that — all things
having been weighed enough, and more — this statement were,
finally, to be established: "*I* am, *I* exist" is necessarily true, so
often as it is uttered by me or conceived by the mind.

[4.] But I do not yet satisfactorily understand who I be, as
that *I* who I now necessarily am. And from the start it is to be
cautioned that I would not perhaps imprudently assume something else in place of me and thus err off even in that cognition
which I contend to be the most certain and the most evident
one of all. Which is why I shall now meditate anew on what
I had once believed myself to be before I have gone into these
cogitations, from which I shall then subtract whatever could
have been weakened even at a minimum by the reasons brought
forth, so that thus, finally, precisely only that which is certain
and unshakeable might remain.

[5.] What, then, have I formerly thought myself to be? Scil.,
a human being. But what is a human being? Shall I say "a
rational animal"? No, because then it would have to be asked
what an animal be, and what rational be, and thus from one
question I would slide down into many and more difficult ones.
Nor do I now have so much leisure that I would want to abuse
it on subtleties of this sort. Rather shall I here pay attention
to what formerly occurred to my cogitation spontaneously and
with nature as a guide whenever I considered what I might
be. Namely, it occurred to me, first, that I had a face, hands,
arms and this whole machine of members such as it also shows
itself in a corpse and which I designated by the term "body".
It occurred to me, in addition, that I was nourished, that I

walked about, that I sensed and that I cogitated: which actions
I referred, of course, to the soul. But what this soul might be,
I did not notice, or else I imagined it as something — I know
not what — exiguous — like a wind, or a fire, or an ether —,
which had been infused into the coarser parts of me. Yet I did
not even doubt about the body, but rather did I think that I
distinctly knew its nature, which — if I had perhaps attempted
to describe it as such as I conceived it with the mind — I would
have explicated thus: By "body" I understand all that which
is fit to be determined by some figure, to be circumscribed by
place, to fill up space in such a way as that all other body be
excluded from it, to be perceived by touch, sight, hearing, taste
or smell, and to be moved in many ways, surely not by itself,
but by whatever else by which it be touched. For I also judged
that to have the power of moving itself, as well as the power
of sensing or of cogitating, in no way pertains to the nature of
a body. Rather was I indeed surprised that such faculties are
found in certain bodies.

[6.] But what am I then now, when I suppose that some very
powerful and, if it is permitted to say so, malign deceiver has —
the effort having been made in all things — deluded me as much
as he could have? Can I affirm that I have even some minimum
of all the things that I have just said to pertain to the nature
of the body? I am paying attention, I am cogitating, I keep
revolving around the same things, and nothing is happening. I
am getting tired of repeating the same things in a frustrating
way. But what about the things that I attributed to the soul? To
be nourished or to walk about? Since I do not now have a body,
these things, too, are nothing but figments. To sense? Of course,
this, too, does not happen without a body, and I have seemed
to sense very many things in dreams that I have then noticed
that I have not sensed. To cogitate? Here I find: it is cogitation;
this alone cannot be rent from me. *I* am, *I* exist; it is certain.
But for how long? So long, of course, as I am cogitating; for it
could perhaps also happen that, if I would cease all cogitation,
I as a whole would at once cease to be. I am now admitting
nothing except what be necessarily true; I am, then, precisely
only a cogitating thing, that is, a mind, or animus, or intellect,
or reason — words with significations previously unknown to

me. But I am a true thing, and truly existing. Yet what kind of thing? I have said: a thinking thing.

[7.] What else am I? I shall imagine: I am not that structure of members which is called "a human body". I am also not some tenuous air infused into these members, not a wind, not a fire, not a vapor, not a breath, not something that I feign to myself: for I have supposed that these things are nothing. There remains the proposition: "*I* am, nonetheless, still something." But perhaps it happens that these things themselves, which I suppose to be nothing because they are unknown to me, would in the truth of the matter still not differ from that me whom I know? I do not know, and I am not now disputing about this matter; I can render judgment only on the things that are known to me. I know that I exist; I am asking who I be, as that *I* whom I know. It is very certain that the knowledge of it — taken thus precisely — does not depend on the things that I do not yet know to exist; and it does not depend, then, on any of the things that I feign with the imagination. And these very words, "I feign", warn me of my error: for I would really and truly be feigning if I were to imagine that I am something, because to imagine is nothing other than to contemplate the figure or image of a corporeal thing. But now I certainly know that I am and simultaneously that it can happen that all these images and whatever things generally are referred to the nature of the body would be nothing but dreams. Which things having been noticed, I seem to be no less inept in saying that I shall imagine in order that I might more distinctly recognize who I might be, than if I were to say that I am indeed already awake and I see something true, but, because I do not yet see it evidently enough, I shall — the effort having been made — fall asleep in order that dreams might more truly and evidently represent this itself to me. Thus do I cognize that none of the things that I can comprehend with the help of the imagination pertains to that knowledge which I have of me, and that the mind is very diligently to be called away from these things in order that it might itself perceive its own nature as distinctly as possible.

[8.] But what, then, am I? A cogitating thing. What is that? A thing doubting, understanding, affirming, denying, willing, not willing, also imagining and sensing, of course.

[9.] These things are indeed many — if they would all pertain to me. But why would they not pertain to me? Is it not *I* myself who am now doubting almost all things, who still understand something, who affirm that this one thing is true, deny the other things, desire to know more things, do not want to be deceived, imagine many things even involuntarily, as well as notice many things coming as though from the senses? What is there of these things that, although I were always sleeping, although he who has created me were even to be deluding me as much as it is in him to do, would not be equally as true as that I am? What is there of these things that might be distinguished from my cogitation? What is there of these things that could be called "separate" from me myself? For that it be *I* who be doubting, who be understanding, who be willing, is so manifest that there might occur to me nothing through which it might be explicated more evidently. But truly *I* am also the same one who imagines. For, although perhaps — as I have supposed — no imagined thing at all be true, the power of imagining itself still really and truly exists, and it makes up a part of my cogitation. Finally, *I* am the same one who senses or who notices corporeal things as though through the senses: viz., I am now seeing light, I am hearing noise, I am sensing warmth. These things are false, for I am sleeping. But certainly I seem to see, to hear, to be warmed. This cannot be false; it is this which in me is properly called "to sense"; and this — taken thus precisely — is nothing other than to cogitate.

[10.] From which things I am indeed beginning to know rather better who I be. But yet it still seems, and I cannot refrain from thinking, that corporeal things — of which the images are formed by cogitation and which the senses themselves explore — are much more distinctly recognized than that of me — I know not what — which does not come under the focus of the imagination. Yet it would be perfectly surprising that things that I notice to be dubious, unknown and alien to me be comprehended more distinctly by me than what is true, than what is cognized and, finally, than me myself. But I see what the problem might be: my mind likes to err off, and it does not suffer itself to be held within the limits of the truth. Let it be, then, and we may once more permit it very lax reins in order

that — these having opportunely been restricted a little later on
— it might suffer itself to be ruled more easily.

[11.] We might consider those things which are commonly
thought to be comprehended most distinctly of all things: scil.,
the bodies that we touch, that we see — surely not bodies in general, for these general perceptions are usually somewhat more
confused, but rather one body in particular. We might take, for
example, this wax here: it has very recently been taken from
the honeycomb; it has not yet lost all the taste of its honey; it
retains some of the odor of the flowers from which it has been
gathered; its color, figure and magnitude are manifest; it is hard,
it is cold, it is easily touched, and, if you were to hit it with a
knuckle, it will emit a sound; in short, all the things are present
in it which seem to be required in order that a body might be
cognized very distinctly. But voilà, while I am speaking, the wax
is moved towards the fire: the remains of the taste are purged,
the odor fades away, the color is changed, the figure is lost, the
magnitude increases, the wax becomes liquid, it becomes hot,
it can hardly be touched, and, if you were to strike it, it will no
longer emit a sound. Does it still remain the same wax? It is to
be conceded that it does remain the same wax. No one denies it
and no one thinks otherwise. What was it, then, in the wax that
was so distinctly comprehended? Certainly none of the things
to which I attained with the senses. For whatever things came
under the scope of taste or smell or sight or touch or hearing
have now been changed: the wax remains.

[12.] Perhaps it — what was so distinctly comprehended in
the wax — was that which I am now cogitating: namely, that
the wax itself has not at all been that sweetness of the honey,
nor that fragrance of the flowers, nor that whiteness, nor that
figure, nor that sound, but rather has it been a body that appeared to me, looked at a little earlier in these ways, and now
in different ways. But what precisely is this that I thus imagine? Let us pay attention to the matter and — the things that
do not pertain to the wax having been removed — let us see
what would remain: obviously nothing other than something
extended, flexible and changeable. But what is this: "flexible"
and "changeable"? Is it what I imagine: that this wax here can
be changed from a round figure into a quadratic one, or from

it into a triangular one? In no way. For I comprehend that the wax is capable of innumerable changes of this kind, and yet I cannot go through innumerable ones by imagining. And this comprehension is not achieved, then, by the faculty of imagining. What is "extended"? Is perhaps the extension itself of the wax also unknown? For in the liquefying wax the extension becomes greater, even greater in the hot one, and greater again if the heat would be increased. And I would not be correctly judging what the wax be unless I did think that it also admits of more variations with respect to extension than I might have ever encompassed by imagining. It remains, then, that I should concede that I do not at all imagine what this wax here be, but rather that I perceive it by the mind alone. I say "this wax here in particular", for it is clearer of wax in general. But what is this wax which is not perceived except by the mind? It is, of course, the same wax that I see, that I touch and that I imagine: the same wax, in short, that I thought it to be from the very beginning. And yet — which is something to be noted — the perception of the wax is not vision, not taction and not imagination, nor has it ever been — although it might previously have seemed so —, but rather is the perception of it the inspection of the mind alone, which inspection can be imperfect and confused — as it was previously — or clear and distinct — as it is now —, depending on how I pay more or less attention to those things of which the wax consists.

[13.] But meanwhile I am surprised at how prone to errors my mind might be. For, although I would consider these things within me tacitly and without a word, I still hang on the words themselves and am almost deceived by the use itself of speech. For we say that we see the wax itself if it be there, and not that we judge from the color or the figure that it is there. From whence I would immediately conclude that, therefore, the wax is cognized by the vision of the eye, not by the inspection of the mind alone — if perhaps I had not now looked out the window at human beings going by in the street, whom themselves I also say, as a matter of the usage of language, that I see, no less than I say, as a matter of the same usage, that I see the wax. But what do I see besides hats and clothes under which automata might be concealed? Yet I judge that there are human beings there. And, thus, that which I thought that I saw with the eyes I comprehend with the faculty of judging alone, which faculty is in my mind.

[14.] But one desiring to know above and beyond the common people should be ashamed to have quested after doubt drawn from the forms of speech that the common people have invented. And let us continue, then, paying attention to the question as to whether *I* more perfectly and more evidently perceived what the wax be, after I have first looked at it and believed that I have cognized it by this external sense — or at least by "the common sense", as they call it, that is, by the imaginative power —, or rather now, however, after I have more diligently investigated both what it might be and how it might be cognized. Certainly it would be inept to doubt about this matter. For what is it that has been distinct in the first perception? What is it which — it would seem — cannot be had by any animal that you will? But truly, when I distinguish the wax from the external forms and consider it — the clothes having been taken off it — as though nude, although there could then yet be error in my judgment, I still cannot thus really and truly perceive it without a human mind.

[15.] But what shall I say about this mind itself, or about me myself? For as yet I admit nothing else to be in me besides a mind. What, I say, *I* who seem to perceive this wax here so distinctly? Perhaps I cognize me myself not only much more truly and much more certainly, but also much more distinctly and much more evidently? For, if from thence that I were to see it, I judge that the wax exists, certainly it is much more evidently effected from thence itself that I were to see it, that I myself also exist. For it can happen that this which I see would not truly be wax; and it can happen that I would not even have eyes with which anything could be seen; but it plainly cannot happen that, when I were to see or (which I do not now distinguish therefrom) when I were to cogitate that I see, *I* myself as the one who is cogitating would not then be something. By similar reasoning, if from thence that I were to touch it, I judge that the wax is, the same thing will again be effected, viz., that I am. If from thence that I were to imagine it, I judge that the wax is, or for any other cause that you will, plainly the same thing will again and again be effected. But the very thing which I notice about the wax may also be applied to all the other things that are posited outside me. Yet, moreover, if the perception of the wax may have seemed more distinct after it had become known to me not by vision or touch alone, but rather by many causes, how much more distinctly — it is to be conceded — am I myself now cognized by me, since no reasoning could aid in the perception of the wax or of any other body that would not — as all the same reasoning — better prove the nature of my mind! But — above and beyond this — there are also so many other things in the mind itself from which the knowledge of it can be rendered more distinct that the things that emanate to it from a body would hardly seem to be worthy to be enumerated.

[16.] And voilà, I have, finally, spontaneously returned to there where I wanted to be. For, because it now be known to me that bodies themselves are properly perceived not by the senses or by the faculty of imagining, but rather by the intellect alone, and that bodies are perceived not from thence that they would be touched or seen, but rather from thence only that they were to be understood, I cognize overtly that nothing can be perceived by me more easily or more evidently than my mind. But, because the custom of an old opinion cannot be laid down so quickly, it is fitting to stop here in order that by the length of meditation this new cognition might be fixed more deeply in my memory.

MEDITATION III.

Concerning God, that he exist.

[1.] Now I shall close my eyes, I shall stop up my ears, I shall call away all my senses, I shall also delete all the images of corporeal things from my cogitation — or rather shall I, because this can hardly be done, certainly regard these images, as empty and false, as being nothing —, and by conversing with and more penetratingly inspecting me alone I shall attempt to render me myself gradually more known and familiar to me. *I* am a cogitating thing, that is, a thing doubting, affirming, denying, understanding a few things, being ignorant of many things, willing, not willing, as well as imagining and sensing. For, as I have noticed before, although those things which I sense or imagine would perhaps be nothing outside me, I am still certain that those modes of cogitating which I call "sensations" and "imaginations", in so far as they are only certain modes of cogitating, are in me.

[2.] And with these few words I have reviewed all the things that I truly know, or at least all the things that I have hitherto noticed that I know. Now I will look around more diligently to see whether there might perhaps be still other things within me at which I have not yet looked. I am certain that I am a cogitating thing. Do I now also know, therefore, what would be required in order that I might be certain of anything? In this primary cognition there is, namely, nothing other than a certain clear and distinct perception of that which I affirm: which would indeed not suffice to render me certain of the truth of the matter if it could ever happen that something that I did so clearly and distinctly perceive were false. And so I now seem to be able to establish as a general rule that all that which I very clearly and distinctly perceive is true.

40

[3.] But yet I have previously admitted many things as completely certain and manifest which later I have still found to be dubious. What kinds of things, therefore, have these been? Obviously the earth, the heavens, the stars and all the other things that I grasped with the senses. But what concerning these things did I clearly perceive? Obviously that the ideas or cogitations themselves of such things were before my mind. Yet not even now am I denying that these ideas are in me. But there was something else that I affirmed and also that — due to the custom of believing it — I thought that I clearly perceived, yet that I did not really and truly perceive, namely, that there were certain things outside me from which those ideas proceeded and to which they were completely similar. And it was in this that I was deceived — or, if I judged the true, it certainly did not happen by virtue of the power of my perception.

[4.] But then what? When I considered something very simple and easy about things arithmetical or geometrical, such as that two and three added together were five, or similar things, did I not then intuit at least these things perspicuously enough that I might affirm that they are true? I have indeed later judged that these things are to be doubted for no other reason than because it came to mind that some God could perhaps have given to me such a nature that I were to be deceived even about those things which would seem most manifest. But, so often as there occurs to me this preconceived opinion about the very high power of God, I cannot not admit that — if he were only to will it — it is easy for him to effect that I would err even in the things that I think that I most evidently intuit with the eyes of the mind. Yet, so often as I turn to those things which I think that I very clearly perceive, I am so fully persuaded by them that I would spontaneously erupt in these words: "Whoever can, may deceive me, he will still never effect that I would be nothing, so long as I shall be cogitating that I am something, or that it would ever be true that I have never been, since it be now true that I am, or even perhaps that two and three added together would be more or less than five, or similar things, in which, scil., I recognize a manifest contradiction." And, since I would have no occasion for thinking that there is a deceiver God, and so far I would not even satisfactorily know whether there be any

God at all, the reason for doubting which depends only on this opinion is certainly very tenuous and — as I would so say — metaphysical.] But, in order that even this reason for doubting might be removed, I ought, as soon as the occasion will occur, to examine whether there be a God, and, if there be, whether he could be a deceiver. For, this matter being unknown, I do not seem to be able ever to be fully certain about any other matter.

[5.] But order now seems to require that I would first classify all my cogitations into certain kinds, and that I would inquire as to in which of them truth or falsity were properly to consist. Some of these cogitations are — as it were — the images of things, which ones alone the term "idea" properly fits: such as then when I cogitate a human being, or a chimera, or heaven, or an angel, or God.] But other cogitations have, in addition, some other forms: such as, when I will, when I fear, when I affirm, when I deny, I surely always then apprehend something as the subject of my cogitation, but by cogitation I also encompass something more than the similitude of that thing. And of these latter cogitations some are called "volitions" or "emotions", but others are called "judgments".

[6.] Now, as for what pertains to ideas, if they were to be regarded solely in themselves and I were not to refer them to something else, they cannot properly be false. For, whether I would imagine a goat or a chimera, it is no less true that I imagine the one than the other. Moreover, no falsity is to be feared in the will itself or in the emotions. For, although I could wish for depraved things, and although I could even wish for those things which nowhere are, it is still not therefore not true that I wish for them. And thus there remain judgments alone in which I have to be cautious in order that I would not be deceived. Furthermore, the foremost and most frequent error that could be found in judgments consists therein that I were to judge that ideas that are in me are similar to — or conform to — certain things posited outside me. For, if I did, in fact, consider these ideas only as certain modes of my cogitation and I did not refer them to anything else, they could hardly give to me any material for erring.

[7.] Furthermore, of the ideas some seem to me to be innate, while others seem to me to be adventicious, and still others seem to me to be made by me. For that I were to understand what a thing be, what truth be and what cogitation be: these things I seem to have not from elsewhere than from my own nature itself. But that I were now to hear a noise, that I were to see the sun and that I were to sense a fire: these things I have hitherto judged to proceed from certain things posited outside me. And sirens, hippogryphs and similar things, finally, are feigned by me myself. Or perhaps I can also think that all these ideas are adventicious, or that all of them are innate, or that all of them are made: for I have not yet clearly seen through to the true origin of them.

[8.] But here it is first and foremost to be asked about the ideas that I consider as though they were derived from things existing outside me what reason would move me in such a way that I would think that those ideas are similar to these things. Obviously I seem to have been thus taught by nature. And, moreover, I know by experience that these ideas do not depend on my will, and, therefore, that they do not depend on me myself. For often these ideas are before me even involuntarily: just as — whether I would want to or not want to — I now sense warmth, and, therefore, I think that this sensation or idea of warmth comes to me from a thing different from me, namely, from the warmth of the fire by which I am sitting. And nothing is more obvious than that I were to judge that that thing immits into me its similitude rather than something else.

[9.] I shall now see whether these reasons be firm enough. When I say here that "I have been thus taught by nature", then do I understand only that I am brought to believe this by a certain spontaneous impetus, not that it is shown to me by some natural light that it is true. Which two things are very different. For whatever things are shown to me by the natural light — such as that from thence that I were to doubt, it would follow that I am, and similar things — can in no mode be dubious, because there can be no other faculty that I could trust equally to that light and that could teach me that such things are not true. But, as for the natural impetuses, already I have often judged earlier that I have then been impelled by them to the worse alternative when it were a matter of choosing the good, and I do not see why I would trust the same impetuses more in any other matter.

[10.] Then again, although these ideas might not depend on my will, it is not therefore so, that they necessarily proceed from things posited outside me. For, just as these impetuses of which I then spoke, although they might be in me, still seem to be different from my will, thus also is there perhaps some other faculty in me which is not yet sufficiently known to me and which is the effecter of these ideas, as it has hitherto always seemed that these ideas are formed in me while I am dreaming and without any help of external things.

[11.] And, finally, although these ideas might proceed from things different from me, it does not from thence follow that those ideas must be similar to these things. Indeed, I seem to have often found a great discrepancy in many things: just as I find within me, for example, two different ideas of the sun, the one, as though derived from the senses, which is maximally to be reckoned among those ideas which I think are adventicious, and through which the sun appears to me to be very small, but the other, derived from the reasoning of astronomy, that is, elicited from certain notions innate to me or made by me in some other manner, and through which the sun is exhibited as being several times greater than the earth. In fact, both these ideas cannot be similar to the same sun existing outside me, and reason persuades me that that one which seems to have emanated from it most proximally is maximally dissimilar to it. = 𝑆𝑒

[12.] All which things satisfactorily demonstrate that I have hitherto believed not by certain judgment, but rather only by some blind impulse, that there exist certain things different from me which would immit ideas or their images into me through the organs of the senses or in some other way whatever.

[13.] But there occurs to me yet a certain other way of inquiring as to whether some of those things whose ideas are in me would exist outside me. To be sure, in so far as these ideas are only certain modes of cogitating, I do not recognize any inequality among them, and they all seem to proceed from me in the same mode. However, in so far as the one idea represents one thing, and the other idea represents another thing, it is obvious that these ideas are very different from one another.

For those ideas which exhibit substances to me are without doubt something greater, and — as I would so speak — they contain more objective reality in themselves, than those ideas which represent only modes or accidents. And, again, that idea through which I understand a highest God — eternal, infinite, omniscient, omnipotent and the creator of all the things that, besides him, are — has, in fact, more objective reality in itself than those ideas through which finite substances are exhibited.

[14.] But now it is manifest by the natural light that there must be at a minimum just as much reality in the efficient and total cause as there is in the effect of the same cause. For from whence, I ask, could the effect get its reality, if not from the cause? And how could the cause give reality to the effect, if it did not also have it? Furthermore, from thence it follows both that something cannot come to be from nothing, and also that that which is more perfect — that is, that which contains in itself more reality — cannot come to be from that which is less perfect. And this is perspicuously true not only of those effects whose reality is actual or formal, but also of ideas, in which only objective reality is considered. That is, for example, not only cannot a stone which has not previously been begin now to be unless it would be produced by something in which there were formally or eminently all that which is posited in the stone; and heat cannot be introduced into a subject that was not previously hot except by a thing that were of an order at least equally as perfect as is the heat, and thus of the other things; but, moreover, even the idea of heat or of a stone cannot be in me unless it had been posited in me by some cause in which there were at a minimum just as much reality as I conceive there to be in the heat or in the stone. For, although this cause were to transfer none of its actual or formal reality into my idea, it is not therefore to be thought that it must be less real, but rather is it to be thought that the nature of that idea is such that of itself it would require no other formal reality besides that which it borrows from my cogitation, whose mode it is. Furthermore, that this idea would contain this or that objective reality rather than some other: this it must, in fact, have from some cause in which there were at a minimum just as much formal reality as this idea contains objective reality. For, if we were to posit that something is found in the idea that had not been in its cause, this it has, then, from nothing. And yet, however imperfect that you will that mode of being might be in which the thing is objectively in the intellect through the idea, it still is, in fact, plainly not nothing, and, therefore, it cannot be from nothing.

[15.] Nor must I suspect that, because the reality that I consider in my ideas be only objective, it is not necessary that the same reality be formally in the causes of these ideas, but rather that it suffices if it were in them, too, objectively. For, just as that objective mode of being belongs to the ideas by the nature of them, so does the formal mode of being belong to the causes of the ideas — at least to the first and foremost ones — by the nature of them. And, although one idea could perhaps arise from another, an infinite regress is still not given here, but rather must it come down, finally, to a primary idea, whose cause would be like an archetype in which all the reality that is in the idea only objectively be contained formally. So that by the natural light it would be perspicuous to me that the ideas in me are like certain images which surely can easily be deficient in the perfection of the things from which they have been derived, but which cannot contain anything greater or more perfect.

[16.] And, the longer and the more curiously I examine all these things, the more clearly and distinctly do I cognize that they are true. But what shall I, finally, conclude from them? Surely that, if the objective reality of any one of my ideas were so great that I would be certain that the same reality is neither formally nor eminently in me, and, therefore, that I myself cannot be the cause of this idea, it necessarily follows therefrom that I am not alone in the world, but rather that there also exists some other thing which is the cause of that idea. But, if no such idea were to be found in me, I shall plainly have no argument that might render me certain about the existence of anything different from me. For I have most diligently looked around at all things and have hitherto been able to find nothing else.

[17.] But of these my ideas, besides that one which exhibits me myself to me — about which there can be no difficulty here —, there is another one, which represents God, there are others, which represent corporeal and inanimate things, others, which represent angels, others, which represent animals, and, finally, others, which represent other human beings similar to me.

[18.] And, as for the ideas that exhibit other human beings, or animals, or angels, I easily understand that they can be composed of the ideas that I have of me myself and of corporeal things and of God, even if there were no human beings besides me, nor animals, nor angels, in the world.

[19.] But, as for the ideas of corporeal things, there occurs in them nothing that would be so great that it would not seem that it can have come from me myself. For, if I were to inspect more penetratingly and were to examine these ideas individually in that manner in which I have yesterday examined the idea of the wax, I notice that there are only very few things in them that I clearly and distinctly perceive: namely, magnitude, or extension in length, breadth and depth; figure, which arises from the determination of this extension; position, which different shaped things obtain among themselves; and movement, or the change of this position; to which can be added substance, duration and number. But the other things, such as light, and colors, sounds, odors, tastes, heat and cold, and other tactile qualities, are not cogitated by me except very confusedly and obscurely — so much so that I even be ignorant as to whether they would be true or false, that is, as to whether the ideas that I have of them would be ideas of certain things, or not of things. For, although shortly previously I might have noted that falsity — properly said, or formal falsity — cannot be found except in judgments, there still is, in fact, a certain other — material — falsity in ideas, then when they represent a non-thing as if it were a thing: just as, for example, the ideas that I have of heat and cold are so little clear and distinct that I could not discern from them whether cold would be only the privation of heat or heat would be only the privation of cold, or whether both of them would be real qualities, or neither would be. And, because there can be no ideas except — as it were — ideas of things, if it would indeed be true that cold is nothing other than the privation of heat, the idea that represents it to me as if it were something real and positive will not without merit be called "false". And thus of the other ideas.

[20.] To which ideas it is, in fact, not necessary that I would assign an author different from me. For, if they would indeed be false, that is, would represent no things, it is known to me by the natural light that they proceed from nothing, that is, that they are in me not for another reason than because something is lacking in my nature and this nature is plainly not perfect. But, if they would be true, because they still exhibit to me so little reality that I could not even distinguish it from a non-thing, I do not see why they could not be from me myself.

[21.] But some of the things that are clear and distinct in the ideas of corporeal things I seem to have been able to borrow from the idea of me myself, namely, substance, duration, number and whatever other things there might be of this kind. For, when I cogitate that a stone is a substance — or that it is a thing that is fit to exist through itself — and also that I am a substance, although I were then to conceive that I am a cogitating and not an extended thing, but that a stone is an extended and not a cogitating thing, and, therefore, that the difference between both these concepts were maximal, they still seem to agree with each other by reason thereof that they both represent a substance. And, when I also perceive that I now am and remember that I have also previously been for some time, and when I have various cogitations whose number I understand, I then acquire the ideas of duration and number, which ideas I can then transfer to whatever other things. But all the other things of which the ideas of corporeal things are made up, namely, extension, figure, position and movement, are surely not contained in me formally, since I be nothing other than a cogitating thing. Yet, because they are only certain modes of a substance — whereas *I* am a substance —, they seem to be able to be contained in me eminently.

[22.] And thus there remains solely the idea of God in which it is to be considered whether there would be something that could not have come from me myself. By the term "God" I understand a substance: a substance infinite, independent, most highly intelligent, most highly powerful, and by which both *I* myself and everything else that is extant — if something else is extant — have been created. All which things are indeed such that, the more diligently I pay attention to them, so much the less would they seem to be able to have come from me alone. And from those things which have been said before it is to be concluded, therefore, that God necessarily exists.

[23.] For, although the idea of substance would surely be in me from thence itself that I be a substance, since I be finite, this idea would, therefore, still not be the idea of an infinite substance unless it did proceed from some other substance which really and truly were infinite.

[24.] And I must not think that I perceive the infinite not through a true idea, but rather only through the negation of the finite, just as I perceive rest and shadows through the negation of movement and of light. For — on the contrary — I manifestly understand that there is more reality in an infinite substance than there is in a finite one, and, therefore, that the perception of the infinite is in me in some mode prior to the perception of the finite, that is, that the perception of God is in me in some mode prior to the perception of me myself. For how would I understand that I doubt and that I desire, that is, that something is lacking in me and that I am not completely perfect, if there were no idea of a more perfect being in me from whose comparison I might recognize my defects? *God*

[25.] And it cannot be said that this idea of God is perhaps materially false and that it can, therefore, be from nothing, just as I have shortly previously noted concerning the ideas of heat and cold and similar things. For, on the contrary, because this idea of God be maximally clear and distinct, and because it contain more objective reality than any other idea, there is no idea more true through itself, nor is there any idea in which less suspicion of falsity would be found. This idea of a most highly perfect and infinite being is, I say, maximally true. For, although it could perhaps be feigned that such a being does not exist, it still cannot be feigned that the idea of it exhibits nothing real to me, just as I have said before of the idea of cold. This idea is also maximally clear and distinct; for whatever I clearly and distinctly perceive that is real and true and that implies some perfection is totally contained in that idea. And it is not an obstacle to this that I would not comprehend the infinite, or that there would be innumerable other things in God that I can in no way either comprehend or even perhaps attain to by cogitation. For it is of the nature of the infinite that it not be comprehended by me, who am finite. And it suffices that I understand this itself, and that I judge that all those things which I clearly perceive and which I know to imply some perfection — and also perhaps innumerable other things of which I am ignorant — are formally or eminently in God, in order that the idea that I have of him might be the maximally true and the maximally clear and distinct idea of all the ideas that are in me.

[26.] But perhaps I am something greater than I myself might understand, and all those perfections which I attribute to God are in some mode in me potentially, even if they themselves had not yet come out and they would not be reduced to act. For I am now getting to know that my cognition is gradually becoming greater, and I do not see what would be an obstacle thereto that it would thus increase more and more into the infinite; and I also do not see why — the cognition having thus increased — I could with the help of it not get all the remaining perfections of God; and, finally, I do not see why the potentiality for producing these perfections, if it is already in me, would not suffice to produce the idea of them.

[27.] But none of these things can be the case. For, first, granted that it be true that my cognition is gradually becoming greater, and that many things are in me potentially that are not yet in me actually, still none of these things pertains to the idea of God — in which surely nothing at all is potential. For this itself — to increase gradually — is a most certain argument for imperfection. Moreover, even if my cognition were always to increase more and more, I understand, nonetheless, that it will never therefore be actually infinite, because it will never be achieved by it that it would not be capable of even greater increase. But I so judge that God is actually infinite that nothing could be added to his perfection. And, finally, I perceive that the objective being of an idea cannot be produced by potential being alone, which is — properly speaking — nothing, but rather can the objective being of an idea be produced only by actual or formal being.

[28.] And there is not, in fact, anything whatsoever in all these things that would not be manifest by the natural light to one who is diligently paying attention. But, because, when I pay less attention, and the images of sensible things blind the vision of the mind, I do not then so easily remember why the idea of a being more perfect than me would necessarily proceed from a being that really and truly be more perfect than me, it is fitting to ask, in addition, whether I — *I* myself as one having this idea — could be, if no such being did exist.

[29.] From whom, then, would I be? Scil., from myself, or from my parents, or from whatever other things less perfect than God. For nothing more perfect than him, nor even anything equally as perfect as he, can be cogitated or feigned.

[30.] But, if I were from me, neither would I doubt, nor would I wish, nor would anything at all be lacking in me. For I would have given to me all the perfections of which there is some idea in me, and thus I myself would be God. And I must not think that those things which are lacking in me can perhaps be more difficult to acquire than those things which are in me now. For — on the contrary — it is manifest that it would have been more difficult by far that I, that is, a cogitating thing or a cogitating substance, emerge from nothing than that I acquire the cognitions of many things of which I am ignorant, which cognitions are only the accidents of that substance. And, if I were to have that greater thing — that I as a cogitating thing or substance had emerged from nothing — from me, I would certainly not have denied to me at least those things which can be had more easily, but nor would I have denied to me even any other things of those which I perceive to be contained in the idea of God, because surely none of these things seems to me to be more difficult to make. But, if they were more difficult to make, certainly they would also seem to me to be more difficult, if I did indeed have the remaining things that I have from me, because I would know by experience that my power terminates in them.

[31.] And I do not escape the force of these arguments if I were to suppose that I have perhaps always been just as I am now, as if it would therefrom follow that about no author of my existence is to be asked. For, because every lifetime can be divided into innumerable parts — each one of which in no way depends on the others —, it does not follow from thence that I had been shortly before, that I must be now, unless some cause were — as it were — creating me again at this moment, that is, preserving me. For it is perspicuous to one who is paying attention to the nature of time that plainly the same power and action are needed to preserve anything whatever at the individual moments at which it endures which would be needed to create the same thing from anew if it did not yet exist. That preservation differs from creation solely by a distinction of reason, then, would also be one of the things that are manifest by the natural light.

[32.] And thus I must now ask me myself whether I would have some power through which I could effect that I — as that *I* who I am now — am also going to be a little later on. For, since I be nothing other than a cogitating thing — or at least since I be now dealing with precisely only the part of me that is a cogitating thing —, I would without doubt be conscious of it if there were such a power in me. But I also know by experience that there is none, and from thence itself I cognize most evidently that I depend on some being different from me.

[33.] Yet perhaps this being is not God, and I have been produced by my parents or by whatever other causes less perfect than God. But, just as I have already said before, it is perspicuous that there must be at a minimum just as much reality in the cause as there is in the effect. And, therefore, it is to be conceded that, since I be a cogitating thing — and having in me some idea of God —, whatever kind of cause of me would, finally, be assigned, it is also a cogitating thing, and that this cause has the idea of all the perfections that I attribute to God. And, again, it can be asked of this cause whether it would be from itself, or from another cause. For, if this cause would be from itself, it is obvious from the things that have been said that it itself is God, namely, because — since it would have the power of existing through itself — without doubt it also has the power of possessing actually all the perfections the idea of which it has in itself, that is, all the perfections that I conceive to be in God. But, if this cause would be from another, it will in the same manner again be asked of this other cause whether it would be from itself, or from another cause, until it would, finally, come down to the ultimate cause: which will be God.

[34.] For it is obvious enough that no infinite regress can be given here, especially since I be here dealing not only with the cause that has once produced me, but also — maximally — with that cause which is preserving me at the present time.

[35.] And it cannot be feigned that several partial causes have perhaps concurred to effect me, and that from one I have received the idea of one of the perfections that I attribute to God, and from another the idea of another, so that all these perfections would surely be found somewhere in the universe, but not all joined together in some one being, who would be God. For — on the contrary — the unity, the simplicity, or the inseparability of all the things that are in God is one of the foremost perfections that I understand to be in him. And the idea of this unity of all his perfections certainly could not have been posited in me by any cause from which I had not also had the ideas of the other perfections. For it could not have effected that I would understand these perfections as joined together and inseparable unless it had simultaneously effected that I would recognize which perfections they would be.

[36.] Finally, as far as pertains to my parents, even if all the things that I have ever thought about them would be true, they still do not, in fact, preserve me, and they have also not effected me, in so far as I am a cogitating thing, in any manner. Rather have they only posited certain dispositions in that matter in which I have judged that I, that is, a mind — which alone I now accept as me —, am. And, therefore, there can be no difficulty concerning them here. Rather is it completely to be concluded from thence alone that I were to exist, and that an idea of a most perfect being, that is, of God, were to be in me, that it is very evidently demonstrated that God also exists.

[37.] There remains only that I would examine how I have received this idea from God. For I have not derived it from the senses, and it has never come to me as one who is not expecting it, as the ideas of sensible things usually then do when these things occur — or seem to occur — to the external organs of the senses. Nor also has it been feigned by me, for plainly I can subtract nothing from it and add nothing to it. And it remains, therefore, that this idea would be innate in me, just as the idea of me myself is also innate in me.

[38.] And it is surely not surprising that in creating me God has given this idea into me in order that it might be like the mark of an artificer impressed on his work. And there is also no need that that mark would be something different from the work itself. But from this one thing — that God has created me — it is very credible that I have in some manner been made in his image and likeness, and that that likeness, in which the idea of God is contained, is perceived by me through the same faculty through which *I* myself am perceived by me: that is, when I turn the vision of the mind into myself, not only do I then understand that I am a thing incomplete and dependent on another, and a thing indefinitely aspiring to greater and greater, or better, things, but simultaneously I also understand that he on whom I depend has all these greater things in him not just indefinitely and potentially, but rather according to the thing itself infinitely, and thus that he is God. And the total force of the argument lies therein that I would recognize that it cannot happen that I would exist of such a nature of which I am, namely, having the idea of God in me, unless God did also really and truly exist: God, I say, he, the same one of whom the idea is in me, that is, having all those perfections which *I* cannot comprehend, but to which I can in some way attain by cogitation, and being subject to no defects at all. From which things it is obvious enough that God cannot be a deceiver. For it is manifest by the natural light that all fraud and deception depend on some defect.

[39.] But, before I were to examine this more diligently and simultaneously were to inquire into the other truths that can be gathered therefrom, it is here fitting to pause for a while in the contemplation of God himself, to reflect within me on his attributes and to intuit, to admire and to adore the beauty of his immense light, so far as the vision of my darkened mind will be able to bear it. For, just as we believe by faith that the highest felicity of the other life consists solely in this contemplation of the divine majesty, so also do we know by experience that the maximal pleasure of which we would be capable in this life can now be perceived from the same — it is granted — much less perfect contemplation.

MEDITATION IV.

Concerning the true and the false.

[1.] In these days I have thus accustomed myself to leading the mind away from the senses, and I have so accurately noticed that there are very few things about corporeal things that be perceived truly, and that many more things about the human mind — and still many more things about God — are cognized, that now I shall without any difficulty turn cogitation from imaginable things to intelligible things only, and ones separate from all matter. And I have indeed a much more distinct idea of the human mind, in so far as it is a cogitating thing — not extended in length, breadth and depth, and not having anything else from body —, than I have a distinct idea of any corporeal thing. And, when I pay attention thereto that I doubt, or that I am a thing incomplete and dependent, then there occurs to me the clear and distinct idea of an independent and complete being, that is, of God. And from this one thing — that there would be such an idea in me, or that *I* would exist as one having this idea — I so manifestly conclude that God also exists, and that my whole existence depends on him at individual moments, that I might be confident that nothing more evident and nothing more certain can be cognized by the human mind. And now I seem to see a way by which one might get from that contemplation of the true God — in whom, namely, all the treasures of the sciences and of wisdom are hidden — to the cognition of other things.

[2.] For among the first things that I recognize is that it cannot happen that God would ever deceive me. For in all fallacy or deception is to be found some imperfection. And, although to be able to deceive would seem to be an argument for sharpness of wit or power, to will to deceive attests without doubt to malice or weakness, and, therefore, does not befit God.

[3.] Next, I know by experience that there is a certain faculty of judging in me which — like all the other things, too, that are in me — I have certainly received from God. And, since God does not will to deceive me, he has, in fact, not given to me a faculty such that I could ever then err when I use it correctly.

[4.] And there would not remain any doubt about this matter if it did not seem to follow therefrom that I can, then, never err. For, if I have whatever is in me from God, and he would not have given to me any faculty of erring, I do not seem to be able ever to err. And thus, in a word, so long as I cogitate only about God, and I as a whole turn myself to him, I find no cause of error or of falsity. But I know by experience that, soon after I have reverted to cogitating about me, I am, nevertheless, subject to innumerable errors, inquiring into the cause of which I notice that there is before me not only a real and positive idea of God, or of a most highly perfect being, but also — as I would so speak — a certain negative idea of nothing, or of that which is most highly absent from all perfection, and that I am so constituted to be — as it were — a middle something between God and nothing, or between the highest being and non-being, that, in so far as I have been created by the highest being, there were surely nothing in me by which I might be deceived or induced to error, but that, in so far as I also participate in some mode in nothing or in non-being, that is, in so far as I am not the highest being himself and very many things are lacking in me, it is not very surprising that I would be deceived. And thus I certainly understand that error, in so far as it is error, is not something real that would depend on God, but rather that it is only a defect; and, therefore, that to err I do not need some faculty bestowed on me by God to this end, but rather that that I were to err is contingent thereupon that the faculty of judging the true which I have from him not be infinite in me.

[5.] Yet this account is still not entirely satisfactory. For error is not a pure negation, but rather is it a privation, or a lack, of some cognition that should in some mode be in me. And to one who is paying attention to the nature of God it does not seem to be able to happen that he had posited in me a faculty which would not be perfect in its kind, or which would be deprived of some perfection that should be in it. For, if the more skilled the artificer is, the more perfect are the works that were to proceed from him, what can have been made by that highest maker of all things that would not be absolute in all respects? And there is no doubt that God could have created me such that I would never be deceived, and there is also no doubt that he were always to will that which is optimal — the question is: whether, therefore, it is better that I am deceived than that I am not deceived?

[6.] While I am weighing these things more attentively, it occurs to me, first, that it is not something for me to be surprised about if certain things whose reasons I would not understand were to be done by God. And his existence is not therefore to be doubted because I were perhaps to know by experience that there are certain other things that had been made by him, why or how I do not comprehend. For, since I were now to know that my nature is very weak and limited, but that the nature of God is immense, incomprehensible and infinite, from this I also satisfactorily know that he can do innumerable things of the causes of which I be ignorant. And for this one reason do I believe that that whole kind of causes which is usually derived from the end has no use in explaining things physical. For not without rashness do I think that I can investigate the ends of God.

[7.] It occurs to me, also, that, whenever we inquire as to whether the works of God would be perfect, not some one creature separately, but rather the whole universe of things, is to be regarded. For what would perhaps not without merit seem very imperfect if it were alone is, as having the nature of a part in the world, most perfect. And, although from thence that I have willed to doubt all things, I have up until now cognized nothing certainly except that I and God exist, from thence that I have noticed the immense power of God, I still cannot deny that many other things had been made by him — or at least that they could be made by him —, so that *I* would obtain the nature of a part in the universe of things.

[8.] Coming more closely to me and investigating of what kind my errors (which alone argue for some imperfection in me) might be, then, I notice that they depend on two simultaneously concurrent causes, namely, on the faculty of cognizing that is in me and on the faculty of choosing or on the freedom of choice, that is, simultaneously on the intellect and on the will. For through the intellect alone I only perceive the ideas about which I can render a judgment, and no error — properly said — is to be found in it — thus precisely regarded. For, although there would perhaps exist innumerable things of which there are no ideas in me, I am still not — properly speaking — to be called "deprived" of these ideas, but rather am I — negatively — to be called only "destitute" of them, because I can surely offer no argument by which I might prove that God ought to have given to me a greater faculty of cognizing than he may have given to me. And, however skilled that you will I would understand an artificer to be, I still do not therefore think that he ought to have posited in every single one of his works all the perfections that he can posit in some of them. And I also truly cannot complain that I had received from God a will, or freedom of choice, not satisfactorily ample and perfect, for I indeed know by experience that it is circumscribed by no limits. And — which seems to me very much to be noted — there are no other things in me so perfect or so great that I would not understand that they can be yet more perfect or greater. For, if I consider the faculty of understanding, for example, I immediately recognize that it is very exiguous and very finite in me, and I simultaneously form the idea of some other faculty of understanding much greater — indeed maximal and infinite —, and from this itself — that I could form the idea of this faculty — I perceive that it pertains to the nature of God. By the same reasoning, if I were to examine the faculty of remembering or of imagining — or whatever other ones are fitting —, I plainly find none that I would not understand to be tenuous and circumscribed in me, but immense in God. It is the will alone, or the freedom of choice, which I know by experience as being so great in me that I might apprehend an idea of no greater faculty — so much so that it be above all it by reason of which I understand that I bear the image and likeness of God. For, although the will, or the freedom of choice, be without comparison greater in God than in me, both by reason of the cognition and of the power that are joined to it and render it more firm and efficacious, and by reason of the object — because it extends itself to more things —, it still does not seem greater, regarded formally and precisely in itself. The reason is that the will, or the freedom of choice, consists only therein that we could do or not do (that is, affirm or deny, pursue or avoid) the same thing, or better, only therein that we were so to be brought to affirm or to deny, or to pursue or to avoid, that which is proposed to us by the intellect that we would sense that we are determined thereto by no external force. For there is no need that I can be moved to both alternatives in order that I might be free; but rather, on the contrary, the more I tend to one alternative — either because I evidently understand the reason of the true and of the good in it, or because God thus disposes the intimate parts of my cogitation —, the more freely do I choose it. Indeed, neither divine grace nor natural cognition ever diminishes freedom, but rather do they increase and corroborate it. But that indifference which I then experience when there is no reason that impels me to one alternative more than to another is the lowest grade of freedom, and that indifference attests to no perfection in this freedom, but rather only to a defect in cognition, or to some negation. For, if I did always see clearly what be true and good, I would never deliberate about that which were to be judged about or chosen. And thus, although I plainly could be free, I could still never be indifferent.

[9.] But from these things I perceive that the power of willing which I have from God — regarded by itself — is not the cause of my errors, for that power is most ample, and perfect in its kind. And the cause of my errors is also not the power of understanding, for, because I were to have it from God that I would understand, whatever I understand, I understand without doubt correctly; nor can it happen that I would be deceived in it. Wherefrom, therefore, do my errors originate? Surely from this one thing: that, because the will open more widely than the intellect, I do not contain the will within the same limits, but rather do I even extend it to the things that I do not understand. Because the will be indifferent to these things, it easily turns away from the true and the good, and thus both am I deceived and do I sin.

[10.] For example, when in these days I were to examine whether anything would exist in the world, and I were to notice that from thence itself that I were to examine this, it evidently follows that I exist, I cannot indeed then not have judged that that which I so clearly understood was true: not that I had been coerced thereto by some external force, but rather because a great propensity in the will has followed from the great light in the intellect, and thus, the more spontaneously and freely I have believed this, the less I have been indifferent to that itself. But now I not only know that I, in so far as I am a cogitating thing, exist, but also, in addition, there is an idea of corporeal nature before me, and it happens that I would doubt whether the cogitating nature that is in me, or better, that *I* myself am, would be another nature different from that corporeal nature, or whether both are the same. And I suppose that as yet there occurs to my intellect no reason that might persuade me of the one possibility more than of the other. From this itself I am certainly indifferent as to whether to affirm or to deny either the one or the other possibility, or even as to whether to judge nothing about this matter.

[11.] Indeed, this indifference even extends not only to those things about which the intellect cognizes nothing at all, but also to all the things generally that are not perspicuously enough cognized by it at that time itself at which the will deliberates about them. For, although probable conjectures were to pull me to one alternative, the cognition alone that they be only conjectures — but not certain and indubitable reasons — suffices to impel my assent to the contrary. Which I have satisfactorily gotten to know by experience in these days, since I have supposed all those things which I had previously believed as being as true as maximally as possible to be wholly false because of this one thing: that I had found that they can in some mode be doubted.

[12.] But, if I were to refrain from rendering judgment then at least when I do not clearly and distinctly enough perceive what were true, it is clear that I act correctly and that I am not deceived. Yet, if I were to affirm or to deny, I do not then correctly use the freedom of choice: and, if I were to turn myself to that alternative which is false, I would plainly be deceived; but, if I were to embrace the other alternative, I would surely come upon the truth by chance, yet I will not therefore be without fault, because it is manifest by the natural light that the perception of the intellect must always precede the determination of the will. And in this incorrect use of free choice is to be found that privation which has constituted the form of error. The privation is to be found, I say, in the operation itself in so far as it proceeds from me, but not in the faculty that I have received from God, nor even in the operation in so far as it depends on him.

[13.] And indeed I do not have any cause for complaining that God had not given to me a greater power of understanding, or a greater natural light, than he has given to me, because it is of the nature of a finite intellect that it not understand many things, and it is of the nature of a created intellect that it be finite. And it is the case that I would give thanks to him who has never owed me anything for that which he has given to me, but it is not the case that I would think that I have been deprived by him of the things which he has not given to me, or that he has taken them away from me.

[14.] I also do not have any cause for complaining that God had given to me a will opening more widely than the intellect. For, since the will were to consist of only one thing, and — as it were — of an indivisible thing, its nature does not seem to bear that anything could be taken away from it. And indeed, the more ample the will is, the greater thanks do I owe to its giver.

[15.] Finally, I should also not complain that God would concur with me to elicit those acts of the will, or those judgments, in which I am deceived. For these acts, in so far as they depend on God, are completely true and good, and it is in a certain mode a greater perfection in me that I could elicit them than if I could not do so. But the privation, in which alone the formal nature of falsity and of fault consists, needs no concurrence of God, because the privation is not a thing, and — related to him as its cause — it should be called not "a privation", but rather only "a negation". For it is surely no imperfection in God that he had given to me the freedom of assenting to or of not assenting to certain things of which he has not posited a clear and distinct perception in my intellect. But it is without doubt an imperfection in me that I would not use that freedom well, and that I would render judgment about the things that I do not correctly understand. However, I see that it can have easily been done by God that, even if I would remain free and of finite cognition, I would still never err: namely, if he had given into my intellect a clear and distinct perception of all those things about which I would ever be going to deliberate, or if only he had so firmly impressed in the memory that of nothing that I would not clearly and distinctly understand is ever to be judged that I could never forget it. And I easily understand that, in so far as I have the nature of a certain whole, I would have been going to be more perfect than I am now, if I had been made as such by God. But I cannot therefore deny that in a certain mode it be a greater perfection in the total universe of things that certain ones of its parts were not immune from errors, but other ones were so immune, than if all the parts would be wholly similar. And I have no right to complain that God had willed that I play a personal role in the world that is not the foremost and maximally perfect one of all.

[16.] And, besides, even if I could not refrain from errors by that prior mode, which depends on an evident perception of all those things about which is to be deliberated, I can still do so by that other mode, which depends only thereupon that I would remember, whenever the truth of a matter is not transparent, that from rendering judgment is to be refrained. For, although I were to know by experience that there is in me the weakness that I could not always inhere fixed in one and the same cognition, by attentive and frequently repeated meditation I can still effect, whenever the need requires me to do so, that I might remember it, and thus I might acquire a certain habit of not erring.

[17.] Because the maximal and foremost perfection of the human being were to consist in this — in having acquired a certain habit of not erring —, I think that I have gained not a little by today's meditation, in that I had investigated the cause of error and of falsity. And there can surely be no other cause of error and of falsity than the one that I have explicated; for, whenever I so contain the will in the judgments to be rendered that it were to extend itself only to the things that are clearly and distinctly exhibited to it by the intellect, it cannot happen at all that I would err, because every clear and distinct perception is without doubt something, and, therefore, it cannot be from nothing, but rather does it necessarily have God as its author — that most highly perfect God, I say, whom it contradicts to be a deceiver; and, therefore, every clear and distinct perception is without doubt true. Nor have I today learned only against what were to be cautioned by me in order that I might never be deceived, but also I have simultaneously learned what were to be done by me in order that I might reach the truth. For I shall indeed reach the truth, if only I would pay enough attention to all the things that I perfectly understand and I would distinguish these from the other things, which I apprehend more confusedly and more obscurely. At which I shall, henceforth, diligently make an effort.

keep will within limits of understanding.

MEDITATION V.

Concerning the essence of material things;
and again concerning God, that he exist.

[1.] There remain to be investigated by me many things concerning the attributes of God, and many things concerning me myself or the nature of my mind. But I shall perhaps resume these things at another time, and nothing seems to be more urgent now (after I have noticed against what were to be cautioned and what were to be done in order to reach the truth) than that I might try to emerge from the doubts into which I have gone in the previous days and that I might see whether something certain concerning material things could be had.

[2.] And, before I shall inquire as to whether any such things would exist outside me, I must surely consider the ideas of these things, in so far as they are in my cogitation, and see which of these ideas would be distinct and which of them would be confused.

[3.] I distinctly imagine, of course, the quantity that philosophers commonly call "continuous", or the extension of the quantity — or rather the extension of the thing quantified — in length, breadth and depth; in it I enumerate various parts; to these parts I assign whatever magnitudes, figures, positions and local movements, and to these movements I assign whatever durations.

[4.] Not only are these things — thus regarded in general — plainly known and transparent to me, but also by paying attention I perceive, in addition, innumerable particulars concerning figures, concerning number, concerning movement and concerning similar things, particulars whose truth is so overt and consentaneous to my nature that, when I first detect them, I would then seem not so much to learn something new as to remember things that I already knew before, or to notice for the first time things that, although I had not previously turned the gaze of the mind to them, were surely already in me for a long time.

[5.] And what I think is maximally to be considered here is that I find within me innumerable ideas of certain things which, even if they would perhaps exist nowhere outside me, still cannot be said to be nothing. And, although they would in a certain manner be cogitated by me at will, they are still not feigned by me, but rather do they have their own true and immutable natures. So that, when I imagine a triangle, for example, even if such a figure would perhaps exist nowhere in the world outside my cogitation — nor would it have ever existed —, there still is, in fact, a certain determinate nature or essence or form of it, immutable and eternal, which has not been feigned by me, nor does it depend on my mind: as is obvious from thence that various properties could be demonstrated about this triangle, namely, that its three angles be equal to two right ones, that the maximum side be opposite to its maximum angle, and similar things, which properties — whether I would want to or not want to — I now clearly recognize, even if I previously would in no way have then cogitated about them when I have imagined the triangle, nor would they therefore have been feigned by me.

[6.] And it is not relevant to the matter if I were to say that, because I surely have from time to time seen bodies having a triangular figure, that idea of the triangle has perhaps come to me from external things through the organs of the senses. For I can excogitate innumerable other figures about which there can be no suspicion that they had ever slipped into me through the senses, and yet I can demonstrate the various properties of them no less than I can demonstrate those of the triangle. All which properties are surely true, since they are clearly cognized by me, and, therefore, they are something, and not merely nothing; for it is obvious that all that which is true is something; and I have already demonstrated in great detail that all those things which I clearly cognize are true. And, even if I had not demonstrated this, the nature of my mind is certainly such that I, nonetheless, could not not assent to these things — at least so long as I clearly perceive them. And I remember that even before this time, when I would inhere as maximally as possible in the objects of the senses, I have always held truths of this mode — which things, namely, of figures or of numbers or of the other things pertaining to arithmetic or geometry or to pure and abstract mathematics in general, I evidently recognized — to be the most certain ones of all.

[7.] But now, if from thence alone that I could draw the idea of something from my cogitation, it follows that all the things that I clearly and distinctly perceive to pertain to that thing do really and truly pertain to it, then cannot therefrom also an argument be had by which the existence of God might be proved? I certainly find within me the idea of God, namely, the idea of a most highly perfect being, no less than I do the idea of some figure or number. Nor do I understand less clearly and distinctly that it pertains to his nature that he always exist than that that which I demonstrate of some figure or number also pertains to the nature of this figure or number. And, therefore, even if not all the things on which I have meditated in these previous days would be true, the existence of God must be within my reach at a minimum in the same grade of certainty in which mathematical truths have hitherto been.

[8.] Yet at first sight this is surely not completely perspicuous, but rather does it bear the look of some sophism. For, since I be accustomed to distinguish the existence from the essence in all other things, I easily persuade myself that the existence can also be separated from the essence of God, and hence that God can be cogitated as not existing. But to one who is paying attention more diligently it still becomes manifest that the existence can no more be separated from the essence of God than it can be separated from the essence of a triangle that the magnitude of its three angles is equal to two right ones, or than the idea of a valley can be separated from the idea of a mountain — so much so that it would be just as contradictory to cogitate God (that is, a most highly perfect being) in whom existence would be lacking (that is, in whom a perfection would be lacking) as to cogitate a mountain from which a valley would be missing.

[9.] Granted, however, that I could not cogitate God except as existing, just as I could not cogitate a mountain without a valley: yet, just as from thence that I would cogitate a mountain with a valley, it certainly does not therefore follow that there is any mountain in the world, so also from thence that I would cogitate God as existing, it does not seem therefore to follow that God exists. For my cogitation imposes no necessity on the things. And, just as it is permitted to imagine a winged horse, even if no horse would have wings, so also can I perhaps feign existence of God, although no God would exist.

[10.] But there is a sophism hidden here. For from thence that I could not cogitate a mountain except with a valley, it does not follow that a mountain and a valley exist anywhere, but rather only does it follow that a mountain and a valley — whether they would exist or whether they would not exist — cannot mutually be separated from each other. But from thence that I could not cogitate God except as existing, it does follow that existence is inseparable from God, and, therefore, that he does really and truly exist: not that my cogitation would effect this, or that it would impose any necessity on anything, but rather, on the contrary, because the necessity of the thing itself, namely, of the existence of God, determines me to cogitate this. For I am not free to cogitate God without existence (that is, a most highly perfect being without the highest perfection) as I am free to imagine a horse with wings or without wings.

[11.] And here it must not be said that, while it is necessary that I would posit God as existing, after I have posited that he has all perfections, since existence is one of these, yet the prior positing has not been necessary: just as it is not necessary that I think that all quadrilateral figures are inscribed in a circle, but, it having been posited that I would think this, it will be necessary that I admit that a rhombus is inscribed in a circle — which is, however, overtly false. For, although it not be necessary that I would ever come upon any cogitation of God, whenever it pleases me to cogitate about the first and highest being, and to draw the idea of him — as it were — out of the thesaurus of my mind, it is still necessary that I were to attribute all perfections to him, even if I did not then enumerate all of them, nor did I pay attention to them as individual things: which necessity plainly suffices so that afterwards, when I notice that existence is a perfection, I might then correctly conclude that the first and highest being exists. In the same way, it is not necessary that I ever imagine any triangle, yet, whenever I want to consider a rectilinear figure having only three angles, it is necessary that I would attribute to it those things from which it is correctly inferred that its three angles are not greater than two right ones, even if I did not then notice this itself. But, when I examine which figures be inscribed in a circle, it is in no way necessary that I would then think that all quadrilateral ones are of that number. Indeed, I also cannot even feign this itself, so long as I will to admit nothing except what I clearly and distinctly understand. And there is, therefore, a great difference between false suppositions of this mode, and true ideas inborn in me, of which the first and foremost is the idea of God. For I surely understand in many ways that this idea is not something fictitious depending on my cogitation, but rather an image of a true and immutable nature: as, first, because no other thing to whose essence existence would pertain can be excogitated by me besides God alone; then, because I cannot understand two or more Gods of this kind, and because — it having been posited that one God would already exist — I were to see plainly that it is necessary that he had also previously existed from eternity and that he were going to remain into eternity; and, finally, because I were to perceive many other things in God, none of which can be taken away or changed by me.

[12.] But, finally, whichever argument of proof I would use, truly the matter always goes back thereto that solely the things that I clearly and distinctly perceive might fully persuade me. And, although some of the things that I thus perceive would be obvious to everyone, while others, however, are not detected at all except by those people who inspect things more closely and investigate things diligently, after they have been detected, these things are, nevertheless, thought to be not less certain than those things. So that, although in the case of a right-angled triangle it would not so easily appear that the square of the base is equal to the squares of the sides as that this base is opposite to its maximum angle, it is still no less believed after it has once been made transparent. But, as for what pertains to God, if I were not overwhelmed by prejudices, and if the images of sensible things did not beset my cogitation from every side, I would certainly recognize nothing prior to, or more easily than, him. For what is more overt from out of itself than that the highest being is, or that God — to whose essence alone existence pertains — exists?

[13.] And, although an attentive consideration has been needed for me to perceive this itself, yet now not only am I equally as certain of it as of all else that seems most certain, but also I notice, in addition, that the certitude of the other things so depends on this itself that nothing could ever be known perfectly without it.

[14.] For, even if I be of such a nature that, so long as I am very clearly and distinctly perceiving something, I could not not believe that it is true, because I am also of such a nature that I could not always fix the gaze of the mind on the same thing in order to perceive it clearly, and because the memory of a judgment previously made would often then recur when I am no longer paying attention to the reasons because of which I have judged such a thing, other reasons can still be offered which — if I were ignorant of God — would easily throw me off from the opinion, and thus would I never have true and certain knowledge of anything, but rather would I ever have only vague and changeable opinions on everything. Thus, when I am considering the nature of a triangle, for example, it surely then appears most evidently to me — as I am steeped in the principles of geometry — that its three angles are equal to two right ones, and I cannot not believe that this is true, so long as I am paying attention to its demonstration. But, as soon as I have turned the vision of the mind away from the demonstration, even though I might then still remember that I have seen through to it most clearly, it can, nonetheless, easily happen that I would doubt whether it would be true — if I would indeed be ignorant of God. For I can persuade myself that I have been made by nature such that I would from time to time be deceived in the things that I think that I perceive as evidently as possible, then especially when I were to remember that I have often held many things to be true and certain which — led to do so by other reasons — I have afterwards judged to be false.

[15.] But, after I have perceived that there is a God, because I have simultaneously also understood that all the other things depend on him and that he is not a deceiver — and I have therefrom gathered that all those things which I clearly and distinctly perceive are necessarily true —, even if I were no longer to be paying attention to the reasons because of which I have judged that this is true, if only I would remember that I have clearly and distinctly perceived it, no contrary reason can be offered that might impel me to doubt it, but rather do I have true and certain knowledge of it. And this is true not only of this, but also of all the remaining things that I remember that I have at some time demonstrated, such as of geometrical and similar things. For what will now be objected to me? Have I been made such that I would often be deceived? But now I know that I cannot be deceived in the things that I perspicuously understand. Have I on other occasions held many things to be true and certain that I have afterwards found to be false? Yet I had clearly and distinctly perceived none of them, but rather had I — ignorant of this rule of truth — perhaps believed for other reasons, which I later detected to be less firm. What will, therefore, be said? That (just as I recently objected to myself) I am perhaps dreaming, or that all those things which I am now cogitating are no more true than are the ones that occur to someone who is sleeping? Yet even this changes nothing. For, although I were dreaming, if something were evident to my intellect, then it is certainly completely true.

[16.] And thus do I plainly see that the certitude and truth of all knowledge depends on the one cognition of the true God — so much so that, before I would know him, I could have perfectly known nothing about any other thing. But now innumerable things — both of God himself and of other intellectual things, as well as, too, of all that corporeal nature which is the object of pure mathematics — can be fully known by, and certain to, me.

MEDITATION VI.

Concerning the existence of material things,
and the real distinction of the mind from the body.

[1.] It remains that I were to examine whether material things would exist. And I now know at a minimum that they can indeed exist, in so far as they are the object of pure mathematics, since I clearly and distinctly perceive them. For there is no doubt that God be capable of effecting all the things that *I* am capable of perceiving thus. And I have judged that there is nothing that cannot ever be made by God — except because of this: that it would contradict being perceived distinctly by me. Moreover, from the faculty of imagining, which I know by experience that I use while I am turned towards these material things, it seems to follow that they do exist. For, to one who is more attentively considering what it might be, imagination appears to be nothing other than a certain application of the cognitive faculty to a body intimately present to it — and, therefore, existing.

[2.] In order that this might become plain, I first examine the difference that there is between imagination and pure intellection. Namely, when I imagine a triangle, for example, not only do I then understand that it is a figure bounded by three lines, but also I simultaneously intuit these three lines with the vision of the mind as though they were present, and this is what I call "to imagine". But, if I would want to cogitate about a chiliagon, I understand equally as well indeed that it is a figure consisting of a thousand sides as that I understand that a triangle is a figure consisting of three. Yet I do not imagine these thousand sides in the same manner, or intuit them as though they were present. And, although — because of the custom always of imagining something whenever I cogitate about a corporeal thing — I might then perhaps confusedly represent to myself

71

some figure, it is still obvious that this figure is not a chiliagon, because it is in nothing different from the figure that I would also represent to myself if I were to cogitate about a myriagon or about any other figure that you will of many sides. Nor does it help anything at all towards recognizing the properties by which a chiliagon differs from other polygons. But, if the question were about a pentagon, I can surely understand its figure, just as I can understand the figure of a chiliagon, without the help of the imagination. Yet I can also imagine the same figure, scil., by applying the vision of the mind to its five sides and simultaneously to the area contained by them. And here I manifestly notice that for imagining a certain peculiar effort of the mind is needed by me which I do not use for understanding: which new effort of the mind clearly shows the difference between imagination and pure intellection. (understanding)

[3.] In addition to these things, I consider that this power of imagining which is in me, in so far as it differs from the power of understanding, is not required for the essence of me myself, that is, for the essence of my mind. For, although the power of imagining were absent from me, I would without doubt remain, nonetheless, that same one who I am now: from whence it seems to follow that this power depends on something different from me. And I easily understand that, if there were to exist some body to which the mind would so be joined that it might at will apply itself — as it were — to inspect it, it can happen that I would imagine corporeal things through this itself — so much so that this mode of cogitating would differ from pure intellection only therein that the mind, when it understands, would then in some manner turn itself to itself and would regard one of the ideas that are in it itself, but, when it imagines, it would then turn itself to the body and would intuit something in it conforming to an idea understood by itself or perceived by the senses. Easily, I say, do I understand that imagination can thus come about, if the body were indeed to exist. And, because there occurs to me no other way equally as convenient for explicating imagination, I therefrom conjecture probably that the body exists. But I conjecture this only probably, and, although I would accurately investigate all things, I still do not yet see that from the distinct idea of corporeal nature that I find in my imagination any argument can be drawn that would necessarily conclude with the proposition that some body exists.

[4.] Yet, besides that corporeal nature which is the object of pure mathematics, I am accustomed to imagine many other things — such as colors, sounds, tastes, pain and similar things —, but none so distinctly. And, because I perceive these things better by means of the senses — from which they seem to have come through to the imagination with the help of the memory —, in order that I might treat of them more appropriately, with the same effort is also to be dealt with the senses, and it is to be seen whether from the things that are perceived by that mode of cogitating which I call "sensation" I could have a certain argument for the existence of corporeal things.

[5.] And here, to be sure, I shall, first, repeat to myself what those things were which I have previously thought to be true just as they were perceived by the senses, and for what reasons I have thought this; then, I shall also set out the reasons for which I have afterwards called the same things into doubt; and, finally, I shall consider what things were now to be believed by me about the same things.

[6.] First, then, I have sensed that I have a head, hands, feet and other members of which consists this body that I regarded as a part of me, or even perhaps as me as a whole. And I have sensed that this body is situated among many other bodies, by which various accommodating ones, or incommodious ones, it can be affected; and those accommodating ones I measured by a certain sense of pleasure, and these incommodious ones I measured by a certain sense of pain. And besides pain and pleasure I also sensed hunger, thirst and other appetites of this kind in me. And I also sensed certain corporeal propensities to cheerfulness, to sadness, to anger, and other similar emotions. But from outside I sensed, besides the extension and figures and movements of bodies, hardness and heat and other tactile qualities in these bodies as well. And, in addition, I sensed light and colors and odors and tastes and sounds, from whose variety I distinguished the heavens, the earth, the seas and the other bodies, the ones from the others. Because of the ideas of all these qualities, which ideas offered themselves to my cogitation and which alone I properly and immediately sensed, I thought surely not without reason that I sensed certain things plainly different from my cogitation, namely, bodies from which these ideas would proceed. For I knew by experience that these ideas come to me without any consent of mine — so much so that I could not sense any object, although I would want to, unless it were present to the organ of sense, nor could I not then sense it when it was present. And, since the ideas perceived by the senses were much more vivid and express — and in their own mode even more distinct — than any of those ideas which I myself — as one prudent and knowing — feigned by meditating or which I noticed as impressed on my memory, it seemed that it cannot happen that they would proceed from me myself. And it remained, therefore, that these ideas would come to me from some other things. Since I would have no knowledge of these things from elsewhere than from those ideas themselves, nothing else could come to mind for me than that those things are similar to these ideas. And, because I remembered that I have been one who has used the senses earlier than reason, and I saw that the ideas that I myself feigned are not as express as were those which I perceived with the senses — and that most of the former are composed of parts of the latter —, I also easily persuaded myself that I have no idea at all in the intellect which I had not previously had in the senses. Also, not without reason did I think that this body, which by some special right I called "mine", pertains to me more than any other bodies do: for I could not ever be separated from it, as I could be from the others; I sensed all appetites and emotions in it and for it; and, finally, I noticed pain and the excitement of pleasure in its parts, but not in the other bodies posited outside it. But why from that — I know not what — sensation of pain a certain sadness of the mind would follow, and why from the sensation of excitement a certain joy would follow, or why that — I know not what — pulling of the stomach which I call "hunger" would warn me about taking in food, but the dryness of the throat would warn me about taking in drink, and thus of the others, I surely had no other reason except: because I have been thus taught by nature. For there is not any affinity at all (at least that *I* would understand) between that pulling and the volition of taking in food, or between the sensation of a thing bringing in pain and the cogitation of sadness arising from that sensation. But I also seemed to have learned from nature all the other things that I judged about the objects of the senses. For I had persuaded myself that these things are thus before I had weighed out any arguments with which this itself might be proved.

[7.] But afterwards many experiences have little by little weakened all the faith that I had had in the senses. For sometimes both towers that had seemed round from far away appeared square from close up, and very large statues standing on their pinnacles did not seem large to one observing them from the ground. And in innumerable other such things I found that the judgments of the external senses are deceived. And deceived are not only the judgments of the external senses, but also the judgments of the internal senses. For what can be more intimate than pain? And yet I had once heard from those people from whom a leg or an arm had been cut off that it seems to them that they sometimes still sense pain in the part of the body that they lacked. Even in the case of myself, therefore, it did not seem to be fully certain that some member hurts me, although I would sense pain in it. To which experiences I have also recently added two maximally general reasons for doubting: The first reason was that I had believed that I never sense anything while I am awake that I could not also sometimes think that I sense while I am sleeping. And, since I would not believe that those things which I seem to me to sense in dreams come to me from things posited outside me, I did not notice why I would rather believe this about the things that I seem to me to sense while being awake. The other reason was that, since I would still be ignorant of the author of my origin — or at least I were to feign that I am ignorant thereof —, I saw that nothing stands in the way thereof that I had been so constituted by nature that I would be deceived even in the things that appeared to me as most true. And, as far as the reasons by which I had before persuaded myself of the truth of sensible things are concerned, I easily responded to them. For, since I would seem to be impelled by nature to many things from which reason dissuaded me, I thought that the things that are taught by nature are not much to be trusted. And, although the perceptions of the senses might not depend on my will, I did not therefore think that it is to be concluded that they proceed from things different from me, because there can perhaps be some faculty in me myself which is the effecter of them, even if it is not yet known to me.

[8.] But, after I am now beginning to know better both me myself and the author of my origin, I think that surely not all the things that I seem to have from the senses are rashly to be admitted; yet I also think that not all such things are to be called into doubt.

[9.] And, first, because I know that all the things that I clearly and distinctly understand can be made by God just as such as I understand them, it is enough that I could clearly and distinctly understand one thing without another thing in order that I might be certain that the one is different from the other: because it can — at least by God — be posited separately. And it does not matter by which power it would happen that the things be thought as being different. And, therefore, from thence itself that I were to know that I exist, and that meanwhile I were to notice that nothing else at all pertains to my nature or essence except this alone — that I were a cogitating thing —, I correctly conclude that my essence consists in this one thing: that I be a cogitating thing. And, although I might perhaps (or rather, as I shall soon afterwards say, for certain) have a body which is very closely joined to me, because I have — on the one hand — a clear and distinct idea of me myself, in so far as I am only a cogitating thing and not an extended one, and because I have — on the other hand — a distinct idea of [the] body, in so far as it is only an extended thing and not a cogitating one, it is still certain that I am really and truly distinct from my body, and that I can exist without it.

[10.] Moreover, I find in me faculties with certain special modes of cogitating — think of the faculties of imagining and sensing —, without which faculties I can clearly and distinctly understand me as a whole, but I cannot — vice versa — understand them without me, that is, without the understanding substance in which they were. For in their formal concept these faculties include some intellection, from whence I perceive that they are distinguished from me just as modes are distinguished from a thing. I also recognize certain other faculties, such as the faculty of changing places, of taking on various figures, and similar ones, which other faculties surely can no more be understood without some substance in which they were than the preceding ones can be, and hence they, too, cannot exist without it. But it is manifest that these other faculties, if they did indeed exist, must be in a corporeal or extended substance — yet not in an understanding one —, namely, because some extension — yet plainly not any intellection — is contained in the clear and distinct concept of them. But now surely there is in me a certain passive faculty of sensing, or of receiving and cognizing the ideas of sensible things. Yet I would have no use for it unless there did also exist, either in me or in something else, a certain active faculty of producing or effecting these ideas. And surely this active faculty cannot be in me myself, because it plainly presupposes no intellection, and these ideas are then produced when I am not cooperating, but rather often even involuntarily. It remains, therefore, that this faculty be in some substance different from me. And, because all the reality that is objectively in the ideas produced by this faculty must be formally or eminently in that substance different from me (just as I have already noticed above): either this substance is a body or a corporeal nature, in which, namely, all the things that are contained objectively in the ideas are contained formally; or certainly this substance is God or some creature more noble than a body, in which, namely, all the things that are contained objectively in the ideas are contained eminently. But, since God not be a deceiver, it is completely manifest that he immits these ideas into me neither immediately through himself nor even by means of some mediating creature in which their objective reality might be contained not formally, but rather only eminently. For, since he has plainly given to me no faculty with which to recognize this, but rather — on the contrary — a great propensity to believe that these ideas are emitted by corporeal things, I do not see how, if these ideas would be emitted from elsewhere than from corporeal things, it could be understood that God is not a deceiver. And thus corporeal things do exist. Yet perhaps not all corporeal things exist completely just as such as I comprehend them by means of sensation, because this comprehension of the senses is in many respects very obscure and confused. But at least all those things which I clearly and distinctly understand, that is, all the things — generally regarded — that are encompassed in the object of pure mathematics, are in corporeal things.

[11.] But, as for what pertains to the other things, which are only particulars — such as that the sun be of such and such a magnitude or figure, etc. —, or which are less clearly understood — such as light, sound, pain and similar things —, although they might be very dubious and uncertain, this itself — that God not be a deceiver —, and, therefore, that it could not happen that any falsity would be found in my opinions unless there would also be in me some faculty given by God to emend it, still shows me the certain hope of reaching the truth even in them. And there is surely no doubt that all the things that I am taught by nature would have some truth in them. For by "nature regarded generally" I now understand nothing other than God himself — or the coordination of created things established by God —, and by "my nature in particular" I understand nothing other than the complex of all the things that have been given to me by God.

[12.] But there is nothing that this nature would teach me more expressly than that I have a body that is then ill when I sense pain, and that then needs food or drink when I suffer hunger or thirst, and similar things. And I should not doubt, therefore, that there be some truth in this. CONTRDAUS [7]

[13.] By means of these sensations of pain, hunger, thirst, etc., nature also teaches me that I am not merely present to my body just as a sailor is present in a ship, but rather that I am very closely joined to, and — as it were — thoroughly mixed with, it — so much so that I were to compose one thing with it. For otherwise, when the body is hurt, *I* — who am nothing other than a cogitating thing — would then, therefore, not sense pain, but rather would *I* perceive this damage with the pure intellect, just as a sailor perceives it by sight if something in the ship would be broken. And, when the body needs food or drink, I would then expressly understand this itself, not have confused sensations of hunger and thirst. For these sensations of thirst, hunger, pain, etc., are certainly nothing other than certain confused modes of cogitating which have arisen from the union and — as it were — thorough mixture of the mind with the body.

UNIUN OC MIND +BODY

[14.] Moreover, I am also taught by nature that various other bodies exist around my body, some of which bodies are to be pursued, and others of which are to be avoided, by me. And from thence that I were to sense very different colors, sounds, odors, tastes, heat, hardness and similar things, I certainly conclude correctly that there are some variations in the bodies from which these various perceptions of the senses come: variations corresponding to — even if perhaps not similar to — the perceptions. And from thence that certain ones of these perceptions be agreeable to me, and others be disagreeable, it is completely certain that my body — or rather I as a whole, in so far as I am a composite of body and mind — can be affected by various things, accommodating and incommodious, from the surrounding bodies.

[15.] But there are many other things that, even if I would seem to have been taught them by nature, I still have really and truly accepted not from it, but rather from a certain custom of judging inconsiderately, and it happens, therefore, that they are easily false: such as that all space in which there occurs nothing at all that were to move my senses would be empty; for example, that in a hot body there would be something completely similar to the idea of heat that is in me, that in a white or green body there would be the same whiteness or greenness that I sense, that in a bitter or sweet body there would be the same taste, and thus of the other things; also, that the stars and towers, and whatever other remote bodies that you will, would be only of the magnitude and figure that they exhibit to my senses, and other things of this sort. But, in order that I might not perceive something in this matter not distinctly enough, I should define more accurately what I would then properly understand when I say that "I am taught something by nature". Here, namely, I take "nature" more strictly than just as the complex of all the things that have been given to me by God. For there are many things contained in this complex that pertain to the mind alone, such as that I were to perceive that that which has been done cannot be made undone, and all the other things that are known by the natural light, concerning which there is no talk here. There are also many things contained in this complex that pertain to the body alone, such as that it

were to tend downwards, and similar things, with which I am
also not dealing. Rather am I dealing only with the things that
have been given by God to me just as a composite of mind and
body. This nature, then, teaches me indeed to flee the things
that induce a sensation of pain, and to pursue the things that
induce a sensation of pleasure, and such things. But it does not
appear that this nature teaches us, in addition, that from these
perceptions of the senses we should conclude anything about
the things posited outside us without the previous examination
of the intellect, because to know the truth about these things
seems to pertain to the mind alone, but not to the composite.
Thus, although a star would affect my eye no more than the fire
of a small torch would, there is still no real or positive propensity in me to believe that the former is no bigger than the latter,
but rather have I from my youth onwards judged this without
reason. And, although I, going to the fire, sense heat, just as I,
going too close to it, also sense pain, there is, in fact, no reason that would persuade me that there is something in the fire
similar to that heat, just as there is, in fact, also no reason that
would persuade me that there is something in the fire similar to
that pain. Rather is there only reason for being persuaded that
there is something in the fire — whatever it would finally be —
that would effect these sensations of heat or pain in us. And, although in some space there were also nothing that would move
the senses, it does not follow that there is, therefore, no body in
it. Rather do I see that in these and in very many other things
I have been accustomed to pervert the order of nature, namely,
because I use the perceptions of the senses, which perceptions
have — properly speaking — been given to me by nature only
to signify to the mind which things would be accommodating
or incommodious to the composite of which it is a part, and
which perceptions are, to this extent, clear and distinct enough,
as certain rules for discerning immediately what the essence of
the bodies posited outside us might be — concerning which
essence, however, these perceptions signify only very obscurely
and confusedly.

[16.] But now I have already satisfactorily seen through to
how — notwithstanding the goodness of God — it would happen that my judgments are false. Yet here there occurs to me

a new difficulty, a difficulty concerning those things themselves which are exhibited to me by nature as things to be pursued or as things to be avoided, and also concerning the internal senses, in which I seem to have found errors: such as when someone — deluded by the pleasant taste of some food — then takes in the poison hidden therein. But then he is indeed impelled by nature only to desire that thing in which there is the pleasant taste, yet not to desire the poison, of which he is plainly ignorant. And nothing can therefrom be concluded other than that this nature is not omniscient: which is not surprising, because, since the human being be a limited thing, no nature would be fitting to that being other than one of limited perfection.

[17.] But truly do we not rarely err even in the things to which we are impelled by nature: such as when those people who are sick then desire drink or food that shortly afterwards is going to harm them. Here it will perhaps be able to be said that these people err due thereto that their nature would be corrupt. But this does not remove the difficulty, because a sick human being is no less truly a creature of God than a healthy one is, and, therefore, it seems to be no less contradictory to suppose that he has a deceptive nature from God. And, just as a clock made up of wheels and weights observes all the laws of nature no less accurately then when it has been fabricated badly and does not correctly indicate the hours than then when it satisfies the wish of the artificer in every respect: so, too, if I were to consider the body of a human being — in so far as it is a kind of machine so fitted out with and composed of bones, nerves, muscles, veins, blood and skin that, even if no mind would exist in it, it would still have all the same movements which in it now proceed not from the command of the will, and thus not from the mind —, I easily recognize that it will be equally as natural for this body that, if it would suffer from dropsy, for example, it suffers a dryness of the throat which usually brings the sensation of thirst to the mind — and also that its nerves and other parts are so disposed by it that it would take in drink, as a result of which the sickness would become greater —, as that, when there is no such mistake in it, it is then moved by a similar dryness of the throat to take in drink useful to it. And, although — regarding the preconceived use of the clock — I could say that, when it does not correctly indicate the hours, it then turns away from its nature, and in the same mode — considering the machine of the human body as prepared for the movements that usually happen in it — I would think that it, too, errs off from its nature if its throat would then be dry when drinking is not beneficial to its preservation, still I notice well enough that this last meaning of the expression "nature" differs a lot from the other meaning of the expression: for this last meaning of the expression "nature" is nothing other than a denomination depending on my cogitation — my cogitation comparing a sick human being and a badly fabricated clock with the idea of a healthy human being and of a correctly made clock — and a denomination being extrinsic to the things of which it is said. But by the word "nature" in the other sense I understand something that is really and truly to be found in the things, and, therefore, it has some truth in it.

[18.] And certainly, even if with respect to the body suffering from dropsy it would be only an extrinsic denomination when from thence that it were to have a dry throat yet would not need a drink, it is then said that "its nature is corrupt", with respect to the composite, or the mind united to such a body, it is still not a pure denomination — but rather a true error of nature — that it would then thirst when drink is going to harm it. Therefore, there here remains to be inquired as to how the goodness of God would not prevent the possibility that nature — so taken — be deceptive.

[19.] Now among the first things that I notice here is that there is a great difference between the mind and the body consisting therein that by its nature the body be always divisible, but the mind be completely indivisible. For surely, when I consider the mind, or me myself in so far as I am only a cogitating thing, I can then distinguish no parts in me, but rather do I understand that I am plainly a thing one and complete. And, although the whole mind would seem to be united to the whole body, I still cognize that, a foot or an arm or whichever other part of the body that you will having been cut off, nothing has therefore been taken away from the mind. And the faculties of willing, of sensing, of understanding, etc., can also not be called its "parts", because it is one and the same mind which wills, which senses and which understands. But — on the contrary — there is no corporeal or extended thing that can be cogitated by me which I might not easily divide into parts by cogitation, and by means of this itself I may understand that it is divisible: which one thing would suffice to teach me that the mind is completely different from the body, if I did not yet satisfactorily know it from elsewhere.

[20.] I then notice that the mind is immediately affected not by all the parts of the body, but rather only by the brain, or even perhaps only by one small part of the brain, namely, by the part in which it is said that the common sense is: which part, as often as it is disposed in the same mode, exhibits the same thing to the mind, even if the other parts of the body could meanwhile have put themselves into different modes — just as innumerable experiments prove, which there is no need to review here.

[21.] In addition, I notice that the nature of the body is such that no part of it could be moved by another part, some distance remote, unless it could also be moved in the same manner by any of the parts that are in between, although the more remote part would do nothing: just as in a cord ABCD, for example, if its last part, D, were to be pulled, the first part, A, will not otherwise be moved than it could also be moved if one of the intermediate parts, B or C, were to be pulled, and the last part, D, were to remain unmoved. And by not dissimilar reasoning, when I sense a pain of the foot, physics has taught me that this sensation then happens by means of nerves distributed throughout the foot, nerves which, extended like cords from there to the brain, when they are pulled in the foot, then also pull the intimate parts of the brain to which they stretch and excite a certain movement in them: which has been established by nature in order that it would affect the mind with a sensation of pain — as it were — existing in the foot. But, because these nerves must pass through the tibia, the thigh, the loins, the back and the neck in order that they would come from the foot through to the brain, it can happen that, even if it is not the part of them in the foot, but rather only some one of the intermediate parts of them, which would be touched, plainly that same movement would happen in the brain which happens, the foot having been

84   *Meditations on First Philosophy*

affected badly: from whence it will be necessary that the mind
would sense the same pain. And the same thing is to be thought
about any other sensation.

[22.] Finally, I notice that, since each and every one of the
movements that happen in the part of the brain that immediately affects the mind carries only some one sensation into it,
nothing better in the matter can be excogitated than if, of all
those which it can carry in, each and every such movement were
to carry in the one sensation that is as maximally and as frequently as possible conducive to the preservation of the healthy
human being. But I also notice that experience attests thereto
that such are all the sensations given into us by nature, and,
therefore, that nothing at all is found in them which would not
attest to the power and goodness of God. Thus, for example,
when the nerves that are in the foot are moved violently and
contrary to custom, this their movement, reaching through the
spinal cord to the intimate parts of the brain, there then gives
to the mind a signal to sense something, namely, the pain — as
it were — existing in the foot, by which the mind is excited to
move, as much as it is in its power, away from the cause of the
pain as harmful to the foot. But the nature of the human being
could have been so constituted by God that this same movement
in the brain would exhibit whatever else that you will to the
mind: namely, this movement itself in so far as it is in the brain,
or this movement itself in so far as it is in the foot or in some
one of the intermediate places, or, finally, something else whatever. Yet nothing else would have been equally as conducive to
the preservation of the body. In the same way, when we need
a drink, a certain dryness then arises therefrom in the throat,
moving its nerves, and by means of them moving the interior
parts of the brain. And this movement affects the mind with a
sensation of thirst, because in this whole business there is nothing more useful for us to know than that we would need drink
for the preservation of health. And thus of the other things.

[23.] From which things it is completely manifest that —
notwithstanding the immense goodness of God — the nature
of the human being, as the nature of a composite of mind and
body, cannot not sometimes be deceptive. For, if some cause,
not in the foot, but in whichever other one that you will of the

[left margin annotations]
all impulses transferred to the brain interpreted by mind are sent with the body movement (the impulse cannot be qualified by reason)

parts through which the nerves are extended from the foot to the brain, or even in the brain itself, were to excite fully the same movement which is usually excited by the badly affected foot, then the pain will be sensed as if it were in the foot — and the senses will naturally be deceived: because, since that same movement in the brain could not but always carry the same sensation into the mind, and it would usually arise much more frequently from a cause that hurts the foot than from another one existing somewhere else, it is consentaneous to reason that it would always exhibit the pain to the mind as the pain of the foot rather than as a pain of another part. And, if a dryness of the throat would once arise not — as usual — from thence that drink be conducive to the health of the body, but rather from some contrary cause — just as it happens in the case of the human being with dropsy —, it is far better that it then deceive than if — on the contrary — it would always then deceive when the body is well-constituted. And thus of the remaining things.

[24.] And this consideration helps very much, not only in order that I might notice all the errors to which my nature is subject, but also in order that I could easily either emend or avoid them. For, because I would know that all the senses indicate the true much more frequently than the false about the things that concern the advantage of the body, and because I could almost always use several of these senses to examine the same thing, and because I could use, in addition, the memory — which connects present things with preceding ones — and the intellect — which has now seen through all the causes of erring —, I should surely no longer fear that those things which are daily exhibited to me by the senses would be false, but rather are the hyperbolic doubts of the last days to be dismissed as worthy of derision — especially the most general one, the one about sleep, which I did not distinguish from being awake. For I now notice that there is a very great difference between the two consisting therein that dreams may never be joined by the memory to all the other actions of life, as are the things that occur to one who is awake. For surely, if, while I am awake, someone were suddenly to appear to me and were immediately afterwards to disappear, just as it happens in dreams, so that, scil., I would see neither wherefrom he had come nor whither he might go, not without merit would I judge that he is a ghost, or a phantasm feigned in my brain, rather than a true human being. But, when the things occur concerning which I distinctly notice wherefrom, where and when they would come to me, and I connect the perception of them without any interruption with the whole rest of my life, then am I fully certain that these things occur not in dreams, but rather to one who is awake. Nor should I even at a minimum doubt the truth of these things if, after I have called together all the senses, the memory and the intellect to examine them, nothing were to be announced to me by any of them that would conflict with the others. For from thence that God not be a deceiver, it completely follows that I am not deceived in such things. But, because the necessity of the things to be done does not always allow the time for such an accurate examination, it is to be conceded that human life is often subject to errors concerning particular things, and the weakness of our nature is to be recognized.

SELECTED BIBLIOGRAPHY

The Standard Edition of the *Meditations on First Philosophy*

Descartes, René. *Meditationes de prima philosophia...*, *Oeuvres de Descartes*, Vol. VII, pp. 1-90. Ed. Charles Adam and Paul Tannery. Paris, 1904, etc.

Literature "on" the *Meditations*

Balz, Albert G. A. *Cartesian Studies*. New York, 1951.
Beck, Leslie J. *The Metaphysics of Descartes: A Study of the "Meditations"*. Oxford/New York, 1965.
Butler, R. J. (ed.). *Cartesian Studies*. Oxford, 1972.
Caton, Hiram P. *The Origin of Subjectivity: An Essay on Descartes*. New Haven, Connecticut, 1973.
Cottingham, John. *Descartes*. Cambridge, 1986.
Cronin, Timothy J. *Objective Being in Descartes and in Suarez*. Rome, 1966.
Curley, Edwin M. *Descartes Against the Skeptics*. Cambridge, Massachusetts, 1978.
Doney, Willis (ed.). *Descartes: A Collection of Critical Essays*. Garden City, New York, 1967.
Idem (ed.). *Eternal Truths and The Cartesian Circle: A Collection of Studies*. New York/London, 1987.
Frankfurt, Harry G. *Demons, Dreamers, and Madmen: The Defense of Reason in Descartes's "Meditations"*. Indianapolis, Indiana, 1970.
Gibson, Alexander Boyce. *The Philosophy of Descartes*. London, 1932/New York, 1967.
Hooker, Michael (ed.). *Descartes: Critical and Interpretive Essays*. Baltimore/London, 1978.
Kenny, Anthony. *Descartes: A Study of his Philosophy*. New York, 1968.

Dudley Di/415

Markie, Peter J. *Descartes's Gambit*. Ithaca, New York, 1986.

Rorty, Amélie Oksenberg (ed.). *Essays on Descartes' "Meditations"*. Berkeley/Los Angeles/London, 1986.

Sesonske, Alexander, and Fleming, Noel (eds.). *Meta-Meditations: Studies in Descartes*. Belmont, California, 1965.

Smith, Norman Kemp. *Studies in the Cartesian Philosophy*. London, 1902/New York, 1962.

Idem. *New Studies in the Philosophy of Descartes: Descartes as Pioneer*. London/New York, 1952.

Williams, Bernard. *Descartes: The Project of Pure Enquiry*. London, 1978.

Wilson, Margaret D. *Descartes*. London, 1978/1982.

Standard Bibliographies on the Philosophy of Descartes

Chappell, Vere, and Doney, Willis. *Twenty-five Years of Descartes Scholarship, 1960–1984: A Bibliography*. New York/London, 1987.

Sebba, Gregory. *Bibliographia Cartesiana: A Critical Guide to the Descartes Literature 1800–1960*. The Hague, 1964.

UNIVERSITY OF
WOLVERHAMPTON
DUDLEY CAMPUS LIBRARY